ENERGIZE YOUR SOUL

wellness cuisine for all seasons by

ENERGIZE YOUR SOUL
wellness cuisine for all seasons by Sundara

Published by Trails Books

a Big Earth Publishing company

Boulder, Colorado 80301

1-800-258-5830

E-mail: books@bigearthpublishing.com

www.bigearthpublishing.com

Contributing author Chef John Williams, CEC

Photography by Joseph Leute

Select photos by Steve Eliasen

Cover design by Heidi Michel

Printed in China

Book design by Ann W. Douden

ISBN: 978-1-934553-44-2

Library of Congress Control Number:

MIX
Paper from responsible sources
FSC™ C005413
www.fsc.org

This book is printed on FSC (Forest Stewardship Council) Certified Paper

Contents

Spring

Summer

Fall

Winter

To authentically eat with the seasons, live the seasons.

The philosophy of "eating with the seasons" is one we've embraced from the day we opened our doors at Sundara Inn & Spa some ten years ago. After all, we're in the heart of the heartland, Wisconsin Dells, Wisconsin, where the seasons are as distinct as asparagus, berries, beets, and sweet potatoes. To cook with the seasons is to rejoice in the family farming way of life here.

With this book, we set out to accomplish three things:

- Show you it is possible to prepare fresh wellness cuisine across four seasons even when you live in the Midwest and are beholden to the quirks of Mother Nature.

- Prove "satisfyingly delicious" and "good for you" need not be mutually exclusive pursuits in wellness lifestyle cooking.

- Fulfill the wishes of our guests who've been clamoring for a cookbook.

If you've been a guest of Sundara, you know our theme line is "Energize Your Soul." Think of these recipes as a way to energize your body, which, in turn, will always feed the soul.

The Sundara Spa Culinary Team

The Sundara Kitchen

Our kitchen at Sundara is modest, and we share that with you to reassure you these recipes will work for the home chef. Yet make no mistake, it is a spa kitchen—no deep fryers, no microwaves, no ingredients that require a can opener.

We use seasonally fresh ingredients with an emphasis on organic, sourced locally whenever we can from family-run farms. In fact, our mantra is, "What can we find within sixty miles?"

We partner with a number of CSA (Community Supported Agriculture) farms, with photos from one of our favorites, Orange Cat Community Farm, spiced throughout the book.

We continue to expand our own gardens, too. We started with four small raised beds to grow a mix of herbs and vegetables. Today we have a 2,000-square-foot organic garden right outside our kitchen door.

As seasons and ingredients come and go, so too, do the dishes on our menu.

And yes, we do serve Wisconsin artisan cheeses and microbrews.

About Chef John Williams

He may not be from Wisconsin, but he's a Midwesterner through and through. Growing up in Michigan, his great grandfather owned a Greek restaurant and his grandfather was a meat cutter. He's quick to share that he knew he wanted to be a chef from the tender age of eight, when he asked his mother if he could prepare Duck à l'Orange for the family. (She insisted on chicken.) He holds multiple culinary and hospitality degrees and became a certified executive chef in 2003.

"When I arrived at Sundara, I knew I had arrived at the kind of cooking I always wanted to do. Fresh, flavorful, proportioned, balanced, seasonal, and sourced locally."

Spring: Inspire Your Spirit.

Hope springs eternal with the first signs of spring in Wisconsin. You can inhale it on the fresh breeze. See it in the green haze that softens the landscape. Feel it underfoot as the ground thaws and the soil comes to life. We're always eager to get planting and have a soft spot for heirloom seed varieties. The outdoor dining cabana adjacent to our infinity pool opens, which guests love. More than anything, we're hungry for anything that's ready for early harvest, which usually means greens and beans. Yet, you might say we still have one foot back in the snow, as we use up the last of the winter root cellar reserves.

Spring

BREAKFAST

Honey Yogurt Dip

Serves 2 as an appetizer

2 cups plain organic yogurt
¾ cup honey
1 lemon, zested
1 orange, zested and juiced
1 lime, zested and juiced

Place yogurt in mixing bowl and add honey, mix well. Add fruit zest and juices from the orange and lime. Mix well and chill for 2 hours before serving. Serve with apples, bananas, pears—even vegetables.

BEVERAGES

Spa-Made Ginger Ale

Serves 3–4

Ginger Water

2 cups water

1 cup ginger, peeled, finely grated

Bring water to a boil in a medium saucepan. Add ginger and reduce heat to medium-low and let simmer for 5 minutes. Remove from heat and let sit for 30 minutes. Strain liquid through a fine mesh strainer and discard ginger.

Simple Syrup

1 cup organic cane sugar

1 cup water

In a saucepan add the sugar and water and bring to a boil to dissolve the sugar. Set aside.

To make individual glasses of ginger ale, place in a tall glass:

Ice

½ cup ginger water

⅓ cup simple syrup

½ cup club soda

1 lime wedge, squeezed

Stir with a bar spoon and enjoy.

Passion Fruit Riesling

Serves 6–8

1 bottle sweet Riesling wine, chilled

1 lemon, cut into wedges

1 orange, cut into wedges

1 lime, cut into wedges

2 cups passion fruit juice

2 cups pineapple juice

1 cup ginger ale

1 kiwi fruit, peeled and cut in slices

Place all ingredients in glass pitcher and enjoy.

Fresh Mint Iced Tea

Serves 6–8

1 cup organic cane sugar

1 gallon plus one cup water

1 fresh vanilla bean, cut in half

12 white tea bags

2 cups loosely packed mint leaves

Place sugar and 1 cup water in a medium saucepan and cook until sugar is dissolved. In a separate pot, bring 1 gallon of water and vanilla bean to a boil. Remove from heat and remove the vanilla bean. Add the sugar/water mixture to the water. Place tea bags and mint into a pitcher and pour in the water, let sit for at least 15 minutes. Mint can be removed or left in the pitcher. Serve over ice.

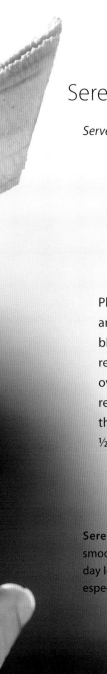

Serenity Smoothie

Serves 1

> 1 mango, cored, peeled, and sliced into chunks
>
> 1 guava, cored, peeled, and sliced into chunks
>
> 1 cup organic pourable vanilla yogurt
>
> ¾ cup pineapple juice

Place the mango, guava, yogurt, and pineapple juice in blender and blend until smooth. For a better result, freeze the mango and guava overnight before adding to the recipe. If you choose not to freeze the fruit beforehand, you may add a ½ cup of ice.

Serenity Smoothie. This is the top-selling smoothie at Sundara and we serve it all day long. Its probiotic qualities make it especially good for digestion.

APPETIZERS

Green and Black Olive Tapenade

Serves 8–12 as an appetizer

- 1 cup pitted green olives
- 1 cup pitted black olives
- 1 anchovy filet
- 2 garlic cloves, crushed with a garlic press or finely chopped
- 2 tsp fresh orange zest
- 2 tsp fresh lemon zest
- 1 Tbsp fresh Italian parsley, chopped
- ½ Tbsp fresh basil, chopped
- ¼ cup extra virgin olive oil
- ¼ tsp freshly ground black pepper

Place olives in a food processor and pulse until coarsely ground. Using flat side of a large knife, mash anchovy with garlic to form a paste. Add anchovy mixture, zest, parsley, basil, oil, and pepper to olives; stir until blended. Serve with crackers, toasted bruschetta bread, or on a muffuletta.

Herb Goat Cheese Spread

Serves 8–12 as an appetizer

- 1 (11 oz) goat cheese log
- 8 oz cream cheese, softened
- 3 Tbsp fresh chives, chopped
- 3 Tbsp fresh parsley, chopped
- 3 Tbsp fresh basil, chopped
- ½ tsp kosher salt
- ⅛ tsp freshly ground black pepper

Place goat cheese and cream cheese in food processor or stand mixer with whip attachment. Whip cheeses together until well incorporated. Fold in the herbs and spices with a rubber spatula. This recipe is great for spreading on crackers, as a vegetable dip, or for adding to tomato soup.

Spicy Shrimp and Chorizo Flatbread

Serves 8

1 large piece flatbread (Lavash or Flatout works well, too)

2 Tbsp jalapeño cream cheese

4 oz chorizo, cooked and crumbled

1 roasted red bell pepper, seeded and sliced

½ cup fresh mozzarella or shredded mozzarella

4 large fresh shrimp, cut into thirds

Green onions, sliced, for garnish

Preheat oven to 400° F. Place flatbread on cutting board or other smooth service tray that you can slide onto your pizza stone. Spread cream cheese over the entire surface, making sure you cover to the edges; this will ensure the edges do not burn. Sprinkle chorizo over the top of the flatbread, followed by red pepper, mozzarella, and shrimp. Bake on a pizza stone until brown and crispy, approximately 8–10 minutes. Remove from oven, slice, and garnish with sliced green onions.

Stuffed Belgium Endive

Serves 8–12 as an appetizer

8 oz package Organic Valley Neufchatel, room temperature

8 oz Carr Valley Ba Ba Bleu cheese, room temperature

½ cup organic cane sugar

1 tsp cumin

1 Granny Smith apple, cored and chopped

4 heads Belgium endive, separated

2 cups Candied Walnuts (recipe on page 130)

1 bunch red grapes (about 20), cleaned and cut in half

¼ cup honey

Add cheeses to a stand mixer and beat on high for 5 minutes or until smooth. In a separate bowl, mix sugar and cumin together and then add to the mixer. Mix for 1 minute. Add apples and mix for an additional 1 minute or until well blended.

Cut the ends off the endive and separate the leaves. Spread each leaf with the cream cheese/apple mixture and arrange on a platter. Garnish each piece with Candied Walnuts and cut grapes. Warm the honey in a saucepan so it's easier to drizzle over the platter.

Sundara Signature Hummus

Serves 10–12 as an appetizer

1 (29 oz) can chick peas, drained
2 cloves garlic
4 oz Tahini paste
1 lemon, juiced
1 Tbsp water
¾ cup extra virgin olive oil
Kosher salt
Freshly ground black pepper

Place all ingredients into food processor and pulse until smooth and creamy. Season to taste with salt and pepper. Serve with pita bread or organic crackers, cucumbers, tomatoes, or other vegetables.

Sundara Signature Hummus.
There's a really creamy texture to this hummus that feels and tastes good on the tongue. Serve with warm pita triangles, tomatoes, cucumbers, feta cheese, and Kalamata olives—and always squeeze more lemon juice on top.

SOUPS AND SALADS

Asian Chicken Salad

Serves 4

4 skinless chicken breasts, marinated
and grilled

2 cups white cabbage, finely shredded

1 head iceberg lettuce, finely
shredded

16 snow peas, julienned

½ cup fresh cilantro, stems removed
and chopped

1 carrot, shredded using a box grater

1 red pepper, seeded and diced

1 cucumber, peeled, seeded, and
thinly sliced

1 bunch green onions, diced

2 cups cooked wonton strips, divided

1 cup sesame lime dressing (recipe on
page 135)

Grill the marinated chicken until it reaches
an internal temperature of 165 degrees. In a
large salad bowl, combine cabbage, lettuce,
snow peas, cilantro, and carrots; toss well.
Add red peppers, cucumbers, green onions,
and 1 cup of wontons strips. Toss again.
Slice the cooked chicken breasts into
¼-inch slices and add to salad bowl. Pour
sesame lime dressing over salad and toss
until all ingredients are well coated. Divide
salad mixture into 4 bowls and garnish
each one with ¼ cup of remaining cooked
wonton strips.

Chicken Marinade

4 cups pineapple juice

⅓ cup red wine vinegar

1 cup sherry

½ cup granulated sugar

1 cup soy sauce

1 Tbsp garlic, chopped

Place all ingredients into a large bowl
and stir until well mixed. Place chicken
into a shallow pan and pour marinade
over the chicken to cover. Place in
refrigerator and marinate for at least
24 hours.

Chilled Asparagus Salad

Serves 4

6 quarts water

1 Tbsp kosher salt

1 Tbsp organic cane sugar

Ice cubes

16 spears small- to medium-size
   green asparagus, washed and ends
   trimmed

1 lemon, juiced

1 Tbsp white wine vinegar

1 tsp honey

1 Tbsp whole grain mustard

2 Tbsp extra virgin olive oil

Bring the water to a boil in a large pot over medium heat. Add the salt and sugar.

Prepare an ice bath by filling a bowl, large enough to hold the asparagus, with cold water. Add some ice cubes. Plunge the asparagus into the ice bath before cooking. This will help to bring any limp stalks back to life. Remove from the ice bath, plunge into the boiling water and allow to cook for 2–3 minutes. Use a slotted spoon to remove from the water, transferring immediately to the same ice bath.

Dry the stalks once they are removed from the ice bath. Taking care that no water gets into the final salad is the best way to ensure that maximum flavor will be enjoyed.

For the dressing:

In a medium bowl, combine the lemon juice, vinegar, honey, and mustard. Stir to blend. Whisk in the olive oil in an even, steady stream. When all of the oil has been integrated, taste and adjust the seasoning, if needed.

Toss the asparagus with the dressing, place on serving platter.

Cobb Salad with Chive Vinaigrette

Serves 2

10 cups, loosely filled, organic spring
    mix greens

½ cup chive vinaigrette (recipe below)

1 avocado, peeled, seeded, and cubed

10 grape tomatoes, cut in half

2 hard-boiled eggs, peeled and
    chopped

1 small red onion, diced

4 oz cooked pancetta, or 4 slices
    cooked Nueske's bacon

Place spring mix in a large salad bowl
and toss with ½ cup of chive vinaigrette.
Place salad in a long line on a rectangu-
lar platter. Start layering avocado, tomatoes, eggs, and onion from one side to
the other. Sauté the pancetta in a sauté
pan on medium heat to warm. If you are
using bacon, cook bacon on medium
heat until crispy on both sides. Serve
warm on top of the salad. Feel free to
add grilled sliced chicken or tofu.

Chive Vinaigrette

1 tsp grated lemon zest

¼ cup fresh lemon juice

2 Tbsp chives, chopped

1 clove garlic, minced

1 tsp organic cane sugar

¾ cup vegetable oil

Kosher salt

White pepper

Place zest, lemon juice, chives, garlic,
and sugar in mixing bowl and whisk
until well incorporated. Slowly whisk in
oil to form the emulsion. Season with
kosher salt and white pepper to taste.

This vinaigrette separates if kept in
the refrigerator, so shake well before
serving. Store for up to 7 days.

**Cobb Salad with Chive
Vinaigrette.** Two surprises
with our Cobb salad—we use
pancetta instead of bacon
to make it healthier, and we
serve it with a chive vinaigrette
instead of bleu cheese
dressing to make it lighter. The
presentation is still traditional
though, with every ingredient
neatly lined up on the plate.
Early spring greens would be
very nice in this salad.

English Pea Risotto
with Truffle Oil and Stravecchio

Serves 8

8 cups organic vegetable stock

4 Tbsp extra virgin olive oil

1 medium yellow onion, diced

2 cloves garlic, minced

2 cups Arborio rice

1 cup Wollersheim Prairie Fumé or your favorite seyval blanc wine

1 cup English peas, shelled

1 tsp kosher salt

½ tsp white pepper

1 Tbsp truffle oil

½ cup Stravecchio parmesan, freshly sliced

Place vegetable stock in large saucepan and heat to a simmer. Keep warm on the back of the stove. In a large heavy saucepan, pour olive oil and sauté onion and garlic until they turn translucent, approximately 2–4 minutes. Add Arborio rice to the pan, stir with wooden spoon, and cook for another 3 minutes. Add the wine and allow the rice to absorb all the wine. Start adding 1 cup of vegetable stock at a time, waiting for the rice to absorb the stock in between ladles. After you have added all the stock, add the peas and remove from heat and add salt and pepper. Place into a large serving bowl and garnish with truffle oil and freshly shaved Stravecchio parmesan. Serve immediately.

MonaVie® Salad

Serves 2 as side salads

- 4 cups, loosely filled, organic spring mix greens
- 3 Tbsp MonaVie Dressing (recipe below)
- 10–12 blueberries
- 2 Tbsp red onion, julienned
- ¼ cup toasted walnuts
- 1 oz chèvre goat cheese

Place spring mix greens and dressing in a bowl and toss carefully. Transfer to serving plate and add blueberries, red onion, and walnuts. Crumble the goat cheese and sprinkle on top.

MonaVie Dressing

- 6 Tbsp MonaVie juice
- ¼ cup red wine vinegar
- ½ pint blueberries
- ¾ cup canola oil
- Kosher salt
- Freshly ground black pepper

Place first three ingredients into blender and purée. Slowly drizzle in canola oil to emulsify, season with salt and pepper to taste. Refrigerate for up to 7 days.

The Taverna Salad

Serves 4

- 11 oz organic mixed greens
- ¾ cup balsamic vinaigrette (recipe on page 128)
- 1 English cucumber, peeled and cubed
- 1 large vine-ripened tomato, diced
- 1 small red onion, diced
- 4 oz feta cheese, crumbled
- 8 oz kalamata olives, pitted

Place mixed greens into a large mixing bowl and toss with balsamic vinaigrette. Divide lettuce mixture between 4 dinner plates. Top each plate with cucumber, tomato, red onion, feta, and olives.

Orzo Salad with Sweet and Sour Peppers

Orzo Salad with Sweet and Sour Peppers.
The roasted red peppers and red onions
bring out a natural sweetness in this very
clean, light pasta salad. We serve it as a
side but it would be a wonderful entrée
salad as well.

Serves 4

1 cup dry orzo
1 red onion, diced
2 large red bell peppers, diced
2 Tbsp balsamic vinegar
2 Tbsp brown sugar
2 Tbsp fresh basil leaves, julienned
1 pint grape tomatoes, cut in half
8 cups, loosely filled, fresh arugula
Kosher salt and freshly ground black
   pepper to taste

Preheat oven to 350° F. Bring 4
cups of salted water to a boil in
a two-quart saucepan. Add dry
orzo and cook until orzo is cooked
but still al dente. Drain and shock
under cold water. Place red onion,
red bell peppers, balsamic vinegar,
and brown sugar in a mixing bowl
and toss until well coated. Place
mixture on a baking sheet and
cover with tin foil and roast for 25
minutes. Remove from oven and
let cool.

In a large mixing bowl place the
cold orzo pasta, the pepper onion
mix, fresh basil, grape tomatoes,
and arugula. Mix well and season
with salt and pepper to taste.

Spinach Salad with Warm Bacon Dressing

Serves 2

9 oz baby spinach, stems removed

½ cup warm bacon dressing (recipe below)

2 hard-boiled eggs, medium dice

2 Tbsp Candied Walnuts (recipe on page 130)

2 Tbsp sun-dried tomatoes, sliced

Clean spinach, removing stem from each leaf. If you have made the dressing ahead of time, you will need to heat the bacon dressing in a shallow sauté pan on medium heat and stir frequently. You will want to bring the heat up slowly so the dressing doesn't overheat and break.

Place cleaned spinach in large bowl and add warm dressing. Toss well, add remaining ingredients and toss again. Serve immediately.

Warm Bacon Dressing

2 lbs Nueske's bacon, diced ¼-inch thick

1 medium red onion, diced

2 cups organic cane sugar

¼ cup apple cider vinegar

1 tsp fresh squeezed lemon juice

2 cups sour cream

Cook chopped bacon on medium heat in sauté pan until completely cooked. Do not drain. Add red onions and cook until translucent. Add sugar and cook until it dissolves. Remove from heat and add cider vinegar.

Let cool for 20 minutes at room temperature.

Add lemon juice and sour cream. Refrigerate if you are not using right away.

Sundara Caesar Salad with Tofu Dressing

Serves 4

2 heads Romaine lettuce, cored and chopped into medium pieces

¾ cup tofu Caesar dressing (recipe below)

1 cup pita croutons (recipe below)

4 Tbsp grated parmesan

4 lemon wedges

Place romaine into colander and wash with cold water, shake to remove excess water. Place into mixing bowl. Add dressing to the romaine and toss to cover. Add croutons and parmesan and toss again. Separate into four bowls and add a lemon wedge to each bowl.

Tofu Caesar Dressing

1 (16 oz) package tofu, drained

2 Tbsp anchovy paste

3 cloves garlic

3 lemons, zested and juiced

3 Tbsp grated parmesan cheese

¼ cup extra virgin olive oil

½ cup hot water

1 Tbsp kosher salt

1 tsp freshly ground black pepper

Place all ingredients into a food processor and purée until smooth and creamy.

Pita Croutons

2 Tbsp extra virgin olive oil

1 clove fresh garlic, minced

1 tsp fresh or dried oregano

Pinch of kosher salt

Freshly ground black pepper

1 8-inch piece pita bread, cut into ¼-inch squares

Preheat oven to 400° F. Combine olive oil, garlic, oregano, salt, and pepper into mixing bowl.

Mix well. Cut pita bread into ¼-inch squares and add to mixing bowl, toss well. Place croutons on baking pan and bake for 5–7 minutes or until croutons are golden brown.

Sundara Quinoa Salad

Serves 4

1 cup quinoa

3 cups water

½–¾ tsp salt

2 cups English cucumber, medium dice

1 small red onion, finely diced, optional

2 vine-ripened tomatoes, medium dice

1 jalapeño pepper, seeded if desired
and finely chopped

½ cup fresh cilantro, stems removed
and chopped

1 Tbsp red wine vinegar

2 Tbsp fresh lime juice

3 Tbsp extra virgin olive oil

1 avocado, medium dice

Freshly ground black pepper to taste

Quinoa Salad. We think of quinoa as the mother grain of the earth. Add avocado if you like.

Place the quinoa in a bowl and cover with cold water. Let sit for 5 minutes. Drain through a strainer and rinse until the water runs clear. Bring 3 cups water to a boil in a medium saucepan. Add salt and the quinoa. Bring back to a boil, and reduce the heat to low. Cover and simmer 15 minutes or until the quinoa is tender and translucent; each grain should have a little thread. Drain off the water in the pan through a strainer, and return the quinoa to the pan. Cover the pan with a clean dishtowel, replace the lid and allow to sit for 10 minutes. If making for the freezer, uncover and allow to cool, then place in plastic bags. Flatten the bags and seal.

Meanwhile, place the finely diced cucumber in a colander and sprinkle with salt. Toss and allow to sit for 15 minutes. Rinse the cucumber with cold water and drain on paper towels. If using the onion, place in a bowl and cover with cold water. Let sit for 5 minutes, then drain, rinse with cold water and drain on paper towels.

Combine the tomatoes, jalapeño, cilantro, vinegar, lime juice, and olive oil in a bowl. Add the cucumber and onion, season to taste with salt and pepper, and add the quinoa. Toss together, taste, and adjust seasonings. Serve garnished with diced avocado and cilantro sprigs.

Sundara Salad with Maple Blueberry Vinaigrete

Serves 1 as an entrée salad or 2 as side salads

> 4 cups, loosely filled, organic spring mix greens
> 3 Tbsp maple blueberry vinaigrette (recipe below)
> 10–12 fresh blueberries
> 3 Tbsp red onion, julienned
> ¼ cup Candied Walnuts (recipe on page 130)
> 1 oz chèvre goat cheese

Place spring mix greens and vinaigrette in a bowl and toss carefully, transfer to serving plate and add blueberries, red onion, and walnuts. Crumble the goat cheese and sprinkle on top.

Maple Blueberry Vinaigrette

> ½ pint fresh blueberries
> ½ cup maple syrup
> ½ cup red wine vinegar
> 1½ cups blended oil, canola and olive oils
> Kosher salt
> Freshly ground black pepper

Add blueberries, maple syrup, and red wine vinegar to the blender and pulse until well incorporated.

Slowly add the blended oil to the vinaigrette, creating the emulsion. Add salt and pepper to taste. Store and use within 7 days.

ENTRÉES

Grilled Tilapia with Jalapeño Cucumber Slaw

Serves 4

> 1½ lbs fresh tilapia, 6 oz each
> 1 Tbsp Sundara Seasoning (recipe on
>   page 136)
> Jalapeño Cucumber Slaw (recipe
>   below)

Spray each filet with nonstick pan coating spray and sprinkle each side of the tilapia with Sundara Seasoning. Grill filets on each side for 4–5 minutes or until fish has been cooked through.

Garnish with the Jalapeño Cucumber Slaw.

Jalapeño Cucumber Slaw

Serves 4

> 1 lb cucumbers, peeled, seeded, and
>   sliced
> 1 red bell pepper, julienned
> 1 yellow bell pepper, julienned
> 2 jalapeño peppers, seeded and cored,
>   cut into ⅛-inch rings
> 1 small red onion, sliced and separated
>   into rings

For the vinaigrette:

> ½ cup rice vinegar
> 1 Tbsp extra virgin olive oil
> 1 Tbsp organic cane sugar
> ¼ tsp kosher salt
> ¼ tsp cumin, fresh ground
> 2 Tbsp fresh cilantro, stems removed
>   and chopped
> ½ tsp Sriracha hot sauce

Place the sliced cucumbers, bell peppers, jalapeños, and red onions in a stainless mixing bowl. Combine the vinaigrette ingredients in a small mixing bowl and mix with a wire whisk until evenly blended. Pour the vinaigrette over the vegetables and toss until evenly blended. Adjust seasoning with additional kosher salt, if desired. Chill for at least 4 hours before serving.

Lamb Quesadilla

Serves 2 as an appetizer

4 Tbsp Red Onion Jam

¼ cup Lime Sour, garnish, optional

4 oz lamb tenderloin, cooked to desired temperature

¼ tsp Sundara Seasoning (recipe on page 136)

4 Tbsp Herb Goat Cheese Spread (recipe on page 11)

1 large flour tortilla

4 large Medjool dates, pitted and sliced

¼ cup bruschetta tomatoes, for garnish, optional (recipe on page 44)

Prepare Red Onion Jam and Lime Sour.

Sprinkle lamb tenderloin with Sundara Seasoning and grill to an internal temperature of 140–150 degrees. Spread goat cheese spread on the tortilla, slice the lamb and spread out on half the tortilla, add onion jam and dates. Fold in half and press down to make it firm. Cook in a skillet or large sauté pan for 3–4 minutes on each side or until it turns toasty brown on each side. Place on cutting board and cut into 4 pieces, serve with Lime Sour and bruschetta tomatoes if you like.

Red Onion Jam

1 Tbsp unsalted butter

1 red onion, julienned

1 Tbsp organic cane sugar

1 Tbsp balsamic vinegar

Melt butter in a medium sauté pan, add onion and cook until translucent, approximately 3–5 minutes. Add sugar and cook for 5 minutes or until the onions have caramelized. Add balsamic vinegar and cook for an additional 5 minutes. Remove from heat and allow to cool.

Lime Sour

1 cup sour cream

¼ cup fresh cilantro, stems removed and chopped

1 lime, zested and juiced

Add all items to a mixing bowl and blend well.

DESSERT

Crème Brûlée

Serves 4

2 cups heavy cream
¼ cup organic cane sugar, plus 4 Tbsp
1 vanilla bean, scraped of seeds
6 egg yolks
Fresh berries, for garnish
Powdered sugar, for garnish

Preheat oven to 325° F. Heat heavy cream, sugar, and vanilla bean and its seeds in a saucepan until cream is hot. Do not over heat because the cream will rise and boil over. Place egg yolks in a small metal bowl and whisk until pale in color. Slowly add ¼ cup at a time of hot cream mixture into the egg yolks. Once all the hot cream has been added to temper the yolks, pour the mixture back into the saucepan and cook over medium heat until thickened—it should coat the back of a spoon. Strain mixture to remove the vanilla bean pod. Ladle mixture equally between 4 custard dishes and place in a baking pan. Fill the baking pan with water until it reaches half way up the custard dishes. Bake for 30–40 minutes until set. Allow to cool for 4 hours before serving.

Caramelizing: After you have allowed the custards to cool, pour 1 tablespoon of white table sugar over the custard, spreading it out carefully over the top of the custard. Using a kitchen torch, heat the top of the sugar until it turns a nice caramel color. Garnish with fresh berries and powdered sugar.

Pineapple Bread Pudding

Serves 9

½ cup organic unsalted butter

3 cups bread cubes, preferably white

8 eggs

1 cup organic cane sugar

5 cups organic skim milk

Seeds from 1 vanilla bean

½ cup pineapple rum

½ cup shredded coconut

1 cup fresh pineapple, diced

Preheat oven to 350° F. Melt butter in a saucepan on medium heat until melted. Pour the melted butter over the bread cubes and toss until coated. Place bread cubes on a cookie sheet and bake until nicely toasted on all sides, stirring once or twice during cooking.

Lower oven temperature to 300° F. Spray a medium-size oven-safe casserole dish with cooking spray and add the toasted bread cubes to the dish. Mix the remaining ingredients in a separate bowl and pour over the bread cubes. Using your fingers, make sure all bread cubes get submerged and soaked before placing the dish in the oven. Cook for 45–60; center should be firm. Serve warm with a dollop of fresh whipped cream.

Tangerine Tiramisu

Serves 9

6 egg yolks

¾ cup organic cane sugar

⅔ cup whole organic milk

1¼ cups heavy cream

½ tsp vanilla extract

1 lb mascarpone cheese

¼ cup strong brewed coffee, room temperature

½ cup fresh squeezed tangerine juice

2 Tbsp dark rum

2 (12 oz) boxes ladyfinger cookies

1 Tbsp unsweetened cocoa powder

In a medium saucepan, whisk together egg yolks and sugar until well blended. Whisk in milk and cook over medium heat, stirring constantly, until mixture boils. Boil gently for 1 minute, remove from heat and allow to cool slightly. Cover tightly and chill in refrigerator for 1 hour.

In a medium bowl, beat cream with vanilla until stiff peaks form and set aside. Whisk mascarpone into chilled yolk mixture until smooth.

In a small bowl, combine coffee, tangerine juice, and rum. Split ladyfingers in half lengthwise, place in serving dish, and drizzle with coffee mixture.

Arrange half of soaked ladyfingers in bottom of a 7x11-inch dish. Spread half of mascarpone mixture over ladyfingers, then half of whipped cream over that. Repeat layers and sprinkle with cocoa. Cover and refrigerate 4–6 hours, until set.

Summer: Pure Joy.

It's life on the lighter side come summer at Sundara. The berries are plentiful. We're pulling lettuce and spinach from the garden. The menu is loaded with lots of fresh salsas made with heirloom tomatoes and sweet corn relishes galore. And watermelon, in soups with a touch of sea salt, and in drinks, too. While avocados have to be sourced from warmer climes, we add them to the menu for their flavor, versatility, and good-for-you attributes.

Summer

Blueberry Blintzes

Serves 4–6

For the Sauce:

2 cups fresh blueberries

6½ Tbsp granulated sugar

1 Tbsp unsalted butter

2 Tbsp fresh lemon juice

½ tsp cornstarch

Pinch of kosher salt

For the Filling:

16 oz cottage cheese

4 oz cream cheese, softened

½ cup plus 3 Tbsp organic cane sugar

1 vanilla bean, halved lengthwise, seeds scraped and reserved, bean discarded

1 cup fresh blueberries

Package of 10 crêpes

Powdered sugar, for garnish

To make the sauce:

Stir blueberries, sugar, butter, lemon juice, cornstarch, and salt in a medium saucepan over medium-low heat. Bring mixture to a low boil. Reduce heat; simmer, stirring often, until berries begin to break down and release their juices, about 10 minutes. Set aside.

To make the filling:

Purée cottage cheese, cream cheese, sugar, and vanilla seeds in a food processor. Transfer to a medium bowl; stir in blueberries. Set aside.

To assemble:

Spoon 2 heaping Tbsp filling onto crêpe, 1 inch from bottom and sides. Fold bottom over filling. Fold in sides, and roll up. Set aside, seam down. Repeat with remaining crêpes and filling.

For frying:

¼ cup unsalted butter

¼ cup canola oil

Heat the butter and oil in clean pan over medium heat. Fry blintzes, turning once, until golden and crisp, 2–2½ minutes per side. Spoon warm sauce over top and dust with powdered sugar.

Strawberry Stuffed French Toast

Serves 4

½ cup strawberries, diced

½ lb cream cheese, softened

8 slices Texas Toast

4 eggs, beaten

½ cup organic whole milk

1 tsp vanilla extract

1 Tbsp unsalted butter

Powdered sugar, for garnish

Blend strawberries and cream cheese. Spread 4 slices of Texas Toast on one side with strawberry cream cheese mixture. Cover with other piece of Texas Toast forming a sandwich. In a medium-size shallow bowl, beat together the eggs, milk, and vanilla extract. Melt butter in a large heavy skillet over medium-high heat. Dip sandwiches in the egg mixture to coat. Place in the skillet, and cook on both sides until golden brown. Garnish with powdered sugar if you like.

Serve immediately.

Strawberry Stuffed French Toast. Cream cheese isn't just for bagels and cheesecake anymore. Add seasonal fruit like apples or berries to the cream cheese or even candied nuts for another layer of flavor.

BEVERAGES

Bliss Smoothie

Serves 1

 1 banana, peeled
 3 large strawberries, stems removed
 ½ cup fresh blueberries
 ½ cup MonaVie juice (can substitute concord grape juice or Wisconsin Door County cherry juice)
 ½ cup organic soy milk

Place banana, strawberries, blueberries, MonaVie juice, and soy milk in blender and blend until smooth. For a better result, freeze the blueberries, strawberries, and banana overnight before adding to the recipe. If you choose not to freeze the fruit beforehand, you may add a ½ cup of ice.

Blueberry Mojito

Serves 1

 Juice of ½ lime
 6 blueberries
 4 Tbsp blueberry purée
 2 Tbsp Simple Syrup (recipe on page 135)
 6 fresh mint leaves
 Ice
 2 oz pineapple flavored rum
 2 Tbsp club soda
 Lime wedge, for garnish

Squeeze juice from half a lime in a pint glass; add blueberries, blueberry purée, Simple Syrup, and mint to the glass. Muddle until you have mashed all the ingredients together. Fill the glass with ice, add rum and top with soda. Garnish with a lime wedge.

Blueberry Sage Martini

Serves 1

Juice of one lemon
2 Tbsp Simple Syrup (recipe on
    page 135)
2 fresh sage leaves
8 fresh blueberries
Ice
1½ oz lemon flavored vodka
½ oz Triple Sec
Fresh blueberries, for garnish
Lemon twist, for garnish

Place lemon juice, Simple Syrup, sage, and blueberries in the bottom of a mixing glass. Muddle until well blended. Fill with ice and add vodka, Triple Sec, and shake well. Strain into a chilled martini glass and garnish with blueberries and lemon twist.

Peach Bellini

Serves 1

2 Tbsp peach purée
2 oz peach Schnapps
4 Tbsp fresh squeezed orange juice
4 oz Moscato d'Asti
2 cups ice
Orange wheel, for garnish

Place all ingredients into a blender and purée until smooth. Pour into a tall pint or hurricane glass. Garnish with an orange wheel.

Raspberry Chocolate Smoothie

Serves 1

1 cup fresh raspberries

1 banana, peeled

2 Tbsp raw cocoa nibs

½ cup almond milk

1 cup organic pourable
   vanilla yogurt

Place all ingredients into a blender and blend until smooth. For a better result, freeze the banana and raspberries overnight before adding to the recipe. If you choose not to freeze the fruit beforehand, you may add a ½ cup of ice.

Pineapple Mojito

Serves 1

6 mint leaves

2 Tbsp Simple Syrup (recipe on
   page 135)

4 large pineapple chunks

½ lime, squeezed

Ice

2 oz Malibu Pineapple Rum

2 Tbsp pineapple juice

4 Tbsp club soda

Mint sprig, for garnish

Place the mint leaves, simple syrup, and pineapple in the bottom of a glass. Squeeze fresh lime juice into glass and muddle ingredients together. Add ice and top with rum, pineapple juice, and club soda. Garnish with a pineapple chunk and fresh sprig of mint.

Pomegranate Mai Tai

Serves 1

Ice
¼ cup pomegranate juice
¼ cup pineapple juice
1 oz Amaretto
1 oz light rum
2 Tbsp Simple Syrup (recipe on
   page 135)
Orange wheel, for garnish, optional

Fill a bar shaker with ice, add all ingredients and shake vigorously until blended. Pour into a pint glass and top off with ice. Garnish with orange wheel if you like.

Raspberry Lemonade

Serves 4

5 cups water, divided
1 cup organic cane sugar
4 lemons, juiced
1 pint fresh raspberries, plus more
   for garnish
Lemon wedges, for garnish

Place 1 cup of water and sugar in saucepan and cook over medium heat until the sugar is dissolved. Remove from heat and let cool to room temperature. Take the juice of the 4 lemons and the pint of fresh raspberries and purée in a blender until smooth. Place raspberry mixture, sugar mixture, and remaining 4 cups water in a pitcher. Pour into 4 ice-filled glasses and garnish with lemon wedges and raspberries.

Tropic Smoothie

Serves 1

> 1 banana, peeled
> ½ cup coconut milk
> ½ cup fresh pineapple chunks
> ¾ cup pineapple juice

Place banana, coconut milk, fresh pineapple, and pineapple juice in blender and blend until smooth. For a better result, freeze the pineapple and banana overnight before adding to the recipe. If you choose not to freeze the fruit beforehand, you may add a ½ cup of ice.

Watermelon Mint Juice

Serves 4–6

> 1 medium watermelon
> 1 orange, juiced
> ½ cup Simple Syrup (recipe on
>   page 135)
> ½ cup mint leaves, torn into pieces

Peel watermelon and slice into ½-inch pieces. Place watermelon pieces into food processor or blender and purée into smooth pulp. Strain mixture into a pitcher through a fine mesh strainer. Add fresh squeezed orange juice, Simple Syrup, and torn mint leaves. Mix well and pour into ice-filled glasses.

Watermelon Mojito

Serves 1

6 mint leaves

2 Tbsp Simple Syrup (recipe
on page 135)

4 large watermelon chunks

½ lime, squeezed

Ice

2 oz Malibu Pineapple Rum

¼ cup club soda

Mint spring, for garnish

Place mint leaves, Simple
Syrup, and watermelon
in the bottom of a glass.
Squeeze fresh lime juice
into glass and muddle
ingredients together. Add
ice, then rum, and top with
club soda. Garnish with
a watermelon chunk and
mint.

Watermelon Mojito. This drink just says fresh
and summer. Grow your own mint like we do
at Sundara and snip some on the spot.

Cucumber Yogurt Dip

Serves 8–10 as an appetizer

- 1 large cucumber, grated
- 1 tsp salt
- 16 oz Greek-style yogurt
- 2 Tbsp fresh chopped dill
- Kosher salt
- Freshly ground black pepper

This recipe will need to be made 1 day in advance before use. Grate cucumber using a large box grater. Add salt to the grated cucumber and let drain for at least 1 hour to remove excess liquid from the cucumber. Place yogurt into a cheesecloth-lined strainer and let drain overnight. This will remove any excess liquid from the yogurt. The next day place the yogurt, cucumber, and fresh chopped dill into a bowl, stir to blend, and season with salt and pepper to taste.

Cucumber Yogurt Dip. Use it as a spread or dip, it's delicious either way.

Jalapeño Cream Cheese

Serves 8–10

> 3 jalapeño peppers, roasted and seeds removed
> 1 lb cream cheese
> 1 tsp Sundara Seasoning (recipe on page 136)

Combine all ingredients in food processor and pulse until well incorporated. Serve as a dip, or use as a spread on sandwiches.

Jerk Shrimp in Spicy Wisconsin Beer Broth

Serves 2 as an appetizer

> ½ bottle Leinenkugel's Honey Weiss beer
> 4 Tbsp unsalted butter
> 1 clove garlic, minced
> 1 lime, juiced
> 1 scotch bonnet pepper, minced
> 4 whole sprigs fresh thyme leaves
> 1 bunch scallions, sliced
> ¼ tsp allspice
> 1 lb medium-size fresh shrimp, peeled, deveined, and tails removed

Preheat oven to 450° F. Pour beer into a 1-quart baking dish and add remaining ingredients and shrimp. Bake for approximately 6–8 minutes or until shrimp are cooked and the broth is hot. Serve with a warm toasted baguette.

Spa-Made Guacamole

Serves 2–4 as an appetizer

3 avocados

¼ cup red onion, diced

2 Roma tomatoes, seeded and diced

1 clove garlic

2 Tbsp cilantro, stems removed and chopped

1 lime, zested and juiced

1 whole chipotle pepper, diced

Kosher salt

Freshly ground black pepper

Peel and seed the avocados, place in a large bowl and mash with a fork. Add red onion, Roma tomatoes, garlic, cilantro, lime zest and juice. Stir to combine. Add the chipotle pepper (you can add more for more heat). Season to taste with salt and pepper. If you make this ahead of time, make sure to keep covered in the refrigerator until use.

Toasted Eggplant Ratatouille

Serves 6–8

1 large eggplant

1 cup extra virgin olive oil

1 medium onion, coarsely chopped

6 cloves garlic, chopped

3 medium zucchini, cut into ½-inch cubes

2 yellow squash, cut into ½-inch cubes

1 large red bell pepper, seeded and diced

1 large yellow bell pepper, seeded and diced

¼ cup balsamic vinegar

3 beefsteak tomatoes, diced

1 cup prepared marinara sauce

1 Tbsp kosher salt

½ tsp freshly ground black pepper

10 fresh basil leaves, torn

Cut eggplant with skin on into ½-inch cubes. Place olive oil in a large sauté pan. Once oil is hot, add eggplant and cook, stirring frequently until eggplant is nicely toasted on all sides. Remove eggplant with slotted spoon and place on a paper towel–lined plate and set aside.

Place pan back on stove and add onion and garlic and cook until translucent. Add zucchini, yellow squash, and bell peppers and cook until softened, approximately 8–10 minutes. Add balsamic vinegar and cook for 1 minute. Then add diced tomatoes, cooked eggplant, marinara, salt and pepper. Cook for an additional 5 minutes. Add the torn basil to the dish just before serving.

Tomato Basil Bruschetta

Serves 8–12 as an appetizer

6 vine-ripened Roma tomatoes
2 cloves garlic, chopped
3 Tbsp extra virgin olive oil
2¼ tsp balsamic vinegar
2 Tbsp fresh basil, chopped
½ tsp kosher salt
¼ tsp freshly ground black pepper

Cut tomatoes in half lengthwise and using a spoon, scoop out the seeds before dicing. Place all ingredients into a mixing bowl and stir with rubber spatula until well incorporated. Serve on crusty bread.

Tomato Basil Flatbread

Serves 8

1 large piece flatbread (Lavash or Flatout flatbreads work well too)
1 large ball of fresh mozzarella or 4 oz shredded mozzarella
2 vine-ripened Roma tomatoes, sliced thin
2 Tbsp grated Stravecchio cheese
Drizzle of Balsamic Vinegar Reduction (recipe on page 128)
6 basil leaves, julienned
Freshly ground black pepper to taste

Preheat oven to 400° F. Place flatbread on cutting board or other smooth service tray that you can slide onto your pizza stone. Spread mozzarella cheese over the entire surface, making sure you cover it out to the edges; this will help to keep it from burning. Lay slices of tomato over the entire surface of the flatbread, spread Stravecchio cheese over tomatoes. Cook on a pizza stone until brown and crispy, approximately 8–10 minutes. Remove from oven, slice and garnish with balsamic reduction, fresh julienned basil, and pepper.

Tuna Ceviche

Serves 2–4

- 8 oz fresh Sushi-grade ahi or yellow fin tuna, diced
- 1 mango, peeled, seeded, and diced
- ¼ cup red onion, diced
- 1 lime, juiced
- 2 Tbsp fresh cilantro, stems removed, chopped fine
- 1 jalapeño pepper, seeded and diced
- ½ cup coconut milk
- ½ tsp sea salt
- ¼ tsp freshly ground black pepper

Use only the freshest tuna you can find and dice into ¼-inch pieces. Be sure to dice the mango and red onion the same size as the tuna. Place all ingredients into a mixing bowl and mix with a rubber spatula. Place in serving bowl and refrigeratate for 1 hour to chill before serving. Serve on toasted crackers, baguette, cucumbers, or plantain chips.

White Bean Purée

Serves 2–4

- 1 cup dry cannellini beans
- ¼ cup extra virgin olive oil
- 2 Tbsp fresh squeezed lemon juice
- 1 clove garlic, minced
- 1 tsp fresh thyme
- 1 tsp fresh rosemary, chopped
- ½ tsp kosher salt
- ½ tsp freshly ground black pepper

Place beans in a bowl, cover with water, and refrigerate overnight. Drain and rinse the beans, add to a saucepan with 4 cups of water and bring to a boil. Reduce heat and simmer for 1 hour. Drain and rinse beans with cold water. Add all ingredients to a food processor and purée until smooth. Serve with crusty bread or as a dip with fresh vegetables.

Caprese Salad with Oven Roasted Tomatoes

Serves 2

10 oven roasted tomato halves (recipe on page 134)

2 fresh buffalo mozzarella balls

10 fresh basil leaves

2 Tbsp extra virgin olive oil

2 Tbsp white balsamic vinegar

Kosher salt, to taste

Freshly ground black pepper, to taste

Preheat oven to 350° F. Place pre-roasted tomatoes on a cookie sheet and heat in the oven for 10 minutes or until nicely warmed. Cut each buffalo mozzarella ball into 5 pieces. Remove tomatoes from oven, and using tongs, shingle tomatoes and fresh mozzarella, alternating each on a long serving platter. Place a basil leaf in between each tomato and cheese layer. Drizzle olive oil and white balsamic vinegar over salad, and season with salt and pepper.

Note: You can use dark balsamic vinegar if you prefer; we use white at Sundara so it doesn't stain the cheese.

Caprese Salad with Oven Roasted Tomatoes. Roasting the tomatoes brings out the natural sweetness. We serve with small batch artisan Wisconsin cheese and extra virgin olive oil.

Carrot Ginger Soup

Serves 4

6 carrots, washed, peeled, and diced

1 small white onion, diced

2 stalks celery, washed and diced

1 Tbsp fresh ginger, minced

½ tsp ground nutmeg

1 clove garlic, diced

½ tsp kosher salt

¼ tsp freshly ground pepper

1 quart organic vegetable stock

1 Tbsp unsalted butter

1 cup organic soy milk

In a medium pot add carrots, onion, celery, ginger, nutmeg, garlic, salt, pepper, and vegetable stock. Bring to a boil, reduce heat and simmer until carrots are tender. Purée the ingredients with a hand blender until smooth. Whisk in the butter and milk until well incorporated. Garnish with fresh nutmeg.

Chilled Banana Soup

Serves 4

> 3 lbs bananas, peeled and diced
> 1 lemon, juiced
> ¾ cup pineapple juice
> 12 oz plain organic yogurt
> 1½ cups vanilla frozen yogurt
>   or custard
> ¼ cup dark rum
> 2⅓ cups coconut milk
> Toasted coconut, for garnish, optional
>   (recipe on page 134)

Purée all ingredients in a food processor, or place in a large bowl and purée using a hand blender. Garnish with toasted coconut if you want, and serve immediately.

Chilled Peach Soup

Serves 4

> 2½ lbs frozen peaches
> ¾ cup sour cream
> ¾ cup pineapple juice
> 1 cup fresh squeezed orange juice
> ¼ cup fresh squeezed lemon juice
> Organic vanilla yogurt, for garnish,
>   optional
> Fresh mint, for garnish, optional

Place all ingredients in a blender and purée until smooth. Pour into chilled bowls and garnish with vanilla yogurt and mint if you like.

Crab and Mango Salad

Serves 2

2 mangoes, peeled and cut into ½-inch pieces

1 (6 oz) can lump crabmeat

1 English cucumber, peeled and cut into ½-inch pieces

4 Tbsp fresh mint leaves, julienned

1 Tbsp fresh parsley, chopped

Lime Vinaigrette

4 Tbsp canola oil

4 Tbsp fresh squeezed lime juice

⅛ tsp kosher salt

2 Tbsp organic cane sugar

Place mango, crab, cucumber, mint, and parsley in bowl and mix with rubber spatula. In a separate bowl, place canola oil, lime juice, salt, and sugar and whisk with wire whisk until blended.

Pour vinaigrette over salad and toss gently.
Serve immediately.

Gazpacho with Lime Sour Cream

Serves 4

2 large vine-ripened beefsteak tomatoes, chopped

1 large vine-ripened yellow tomato, chopped

1 red bell pepper, chopped

1 green bell pepper, chopped

1 jalapeño, optional

¼ cup fresh cilantro, stems removed and chopped

¼ cup fresh lime juice

2 cups Sundara Bloody Mary Mix (recipe on page 130)

2 English cucumbers, peeled and chopped

2 Tbsp garlic, chopped

1 Tbsp chili powder

Kosher salt, to taste

Freshly ground black pepper, to taste

Lime Sour Cream (recipe below)

Place all ingredients into a food processor and purée until smooth.
Garnish each bowl with a dollop of Lime Sour Cream.

Lime Sour Cream

1 cup sour cream

¼ cup cilantro, stems removed and chopped

1 lime, zested and juiced

Add all ingredients to a mixing bowl and blend well.

Heirloom Tomato Soup with Herb Goat Cheese

Serves 4

2 lbs heirloom varietal tomatoes

2 Tbsp unsalted butter

1 small yellow onion, diced small

1 garlic clove, minced

1 yellow pepper, seeded and diced

2 sprigs fresh oregano

4 cups organic vegetable stock

1 cup heavy cream

3 tsp kosher salt

Freshly ground black pepper to taste

Garnish with a dollop of herb goat cheese, optional (recipe on page 11)

Heirloom Tomato Soup with Herb Goat Cheese. We use heirloom Wisconsin tomatoes grown in our garden for this soup, but plums work well, too.

Remove the core from each tomato by using a paring knife. Now cut a small X in the bottom of each tomato. Bring a medium saucepan filled with water to a boil. Drop each tomato into the boiling water using a slotted spoon for 1 minute, remove from the water with the slotted spoon and set on a towel to cool. You should be able to remove the skin from the tomatoes with ease. Cut each tomato in half and remove the seeds. In a large stockpot add the butter and onion and cook over medium heat until the onions are translucent. Add the garlic and cook for an additional 1 minute. Now add the tomatoes, yellow pepper, and fresh oregano and let the mixture simmer for 5 minutes. Add the vegetable stock and simmer for 15 minutes. Using an immersion blender, purée the mixture until well blended. You can also pour the mixture into a standing blender. After you have blended the soup, add heavy cream, salt, and pepper. Simmer for 10 minutes and serve. Garnish with herb goat cheese if you like.

Seared Scallop Salad with Citrus Poppy Seed Vinaigrette

Serves 4

8 large fresh sea scallops

Kosher salt

Freshly ground black pepper

½ lb fingerling potatoes, each cut in half

6 cups, loosely filled, fresh arugula

24 red grapes, cut in half

4 radishes, sliced thin

2 avocados, peeled and cut into ½-inch pieces

1 cup Citrus Poppy Seed Vinaigrette (recipe opposite)

4 tsp toasted pine nuts

Scallops:

Spray a medium sauté pan with nonstick spray. Sprinkle each scallop with kosher salt and freshly ground black pepper. Sear on each side for 2 minutes, until nicely browned. You want a nice crust on the outside but still medium-rare in the middle. Remove from heat and place in oven to keep warm. Cut each scallop into 4 pieces before serving.

Cook fingerlings in salted boiling water for approximately 8–10 minutes until fully cooked. Strain and set aside.

In a large mixing bowl, place arugula, halved grapes, radishes, fingerlings, and avocados. Add dressing and gently toss. Place on serving platter and place scallops on salad and garnish with toasted pine nuts.

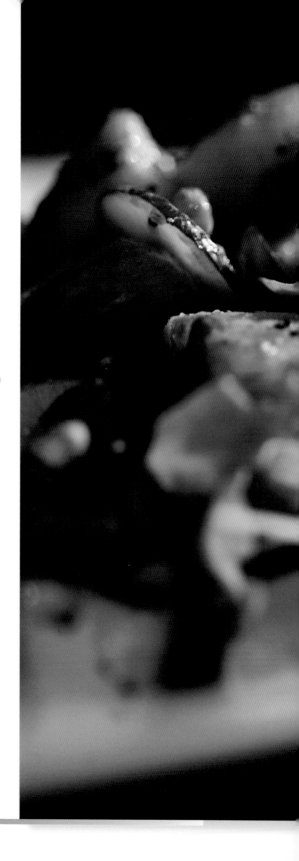

Citrus Poppy Seed Vinaigrette

½ cup fresh squeezed
    orange juice
4 Tbsp white wine vinegar
4 Tbsp fresh scallions, chopped
½ cup organic cane sugar
¼ tsp kosher salt
2 Tbsp poppy seeds
⅔ cup canola oil

Place orange juice, vinegar, scallions, sugar, salt, and poppy seeds into a mixing bowl and whisk until well mixed. Slowly drizzle oil into bowl while whisking to form an emulsion. Store in refrigerator for up to 7 days.

Seared Scallop Salad with Citrus Poppy Seed Vinaigrette. This is a bit of the East Coast brought to landlocked Wisconsin.

Strawberry Fields Salad

Serves 4

11 oz spring mix greens

1 cup Raspberry Vinaigrette

1 cup dried banana chips

1 cup Candied Walnuts (recipe on page 130)

1 pint strawberries, sliced

4 Tbsp toasted coconut (recipe on page 134)

Grilled skinless chicken breasts, optional

Place mixed greens in large mixing bowl and toss with dressing. Distribute salad mixture over 4 dinner plates and garnish with banana chips, Candied Walnuts, strawberries, and toasted coconut. Feel free to add grilled chicken breast, shrimp, or pork loin.

Raspberry Vinaigrette

½ pint fresh raspberries

1 Tbsp Dijon mustard

2 Tbsp freshly squeezed lemon juice

2 Tbsp red wine vinegar

2 Tbsp organic cane sugar

2 Tbsp honey

½ tsp kosher salt

¼ tsp freshly ground black pepper

¾ cup canola oil

Place all ingredients except the canola oil into a blender and blend until smooth. While the motor is running, add the oil in a slow steady stream. This fresh raspberry vinaigrette can be kept in the refrigerator for up to one week.

Strawberry Fields Salad.
Look for little twists to make this
recipe your own. We changed it up
with the addition of banana chips and
toasted coconut.

Sweet Corn Bisque

Serves 8

1 cup Vidalia onion, diced

2 red skin potatoes, diced small
   with skin on

1 Tbsp extra virgin olive oil

2 cups fresh corn kernels

1 tsp garlic, minced

1 Tbsp thyme, dried or fresh

3 Tbsp white unbleached flour

4 cups organic vegetable stock

2 cups soy milk

Kosher salt

Freshly ground black pepper

In a large saucepan, sauté onion and potato in olive oil until onion begins to soften, about 3 minutes. Add corn and garlic and continue to sauté an additional 5 minutes. Add thyme and slowly stir in flour until well incorporated to make a roux. Slowly add stock, stir constantly to prevent lumps. Once all stock is added, bring to a simmer and cook until potatoes are soft, about 30 minutes. Remove from heat, and let cool about 5 minutes. Add soy milk and purée soup in a blender. Add puréed soup back to pan, season with salt and pepper to taste and return to heat.

Sweet Corn Bisque. Good ol' Wisconsin sweet corn is the star here. We use almond milk and vegetable stock to keep it light and vegetarian.

ENTRÉES

Sundara Wrap with Jalapeño Vinaigrette

Serves 2–4

4 cups, loosely filled, organic spring mix greens

1 carrot, cleaned and shredded

1 cup shredded green cabbage

1 bunch green onions, sliced

1 red bell pepper, seeded and sliced

½ cup Jalapeño Vinaigrette (recipe below)

2 large whole grain wheat wraps

Grilled chicken, optional

Place spring mix into a large mixing bowl. Add carrots, cabbage, green onions, and bell pepper and toss gently. Add Jalapeño Vinaigrette and toss again. Divide greens between the two tortillas. Roll the front edge of the tortilla over the greens and tuck it inside. Fold in the sides and roll like a burrito. Cut it in half on the bias and serve.

Jalapeño Vinaigrette

2 jalapeños, chopped

1 bunch cilantro, stems removed

2 cloves garlic

6 Tbsp Dijon mustard

½ cup rice wine vinegar

2 Tbsp organic cane sugar

1¼ cups canola oil

Kosher salt

Freshly ground black pepper

Place all ingredients with the exception of the oil, salt, and pepper into a blender and blend for 30 seconds. While the blender is still on, slowly drizzle in the oil to form the emulsion. Do not add the oil too quickly or you can break apart the vinaigrette. Season to taste with salt and pepper. If you want to cut down on the heat of the vinaigrette, remove the seeds from the jalapeño before adding to the blender. Refrigerate for up to 7 days.

Crab Cakes with Charred Corn Relish and Roasted Pepper Aioli

Serves 10–12

4 (6 oz each) cans crabmeat

4 cloves garlic, minced

1 Tbsp prepared horseradish

1 red bell pepper, seeded and diced

1 bunch scallions, sliced

½ cup fresh cilantro, stems removed and chopped

Juice of 1 lime

2 eggs

1 Tbsp Dijon mustard

1 Tbsp Old Bay seasoning

1 cup panko breadcrumbs

½ cup unsalted butter

Crab Cakes. Our crab cakes are prepared classic Maryland-style and served as an entrée. The charred corn relish is really a standout in this dish—we char the corn right on a grill.

Combine all ingredients in a large metal bowl and mix well. Make sure the crab has loosened up and is not in large clumps. Portion the crab cakes into small balls approximately 3 oz each, about the size of a lime. The best way to cook crab cakes is in a nonstick skillet. Add butter to the bottom of the skillet, turn heat to medium. Brown crab cakes on each side, 4–5 minutes per side. Serve with Red Pepper Aioli and Charred Corn Relish (recipes opposite).

it under water. Place the red pepper into a food processor along with egg yolk, garlic, red wine vinegar, and Tabasco. Purée ingredients for 30 seconds. Slowly pour the oil into the food processor while it's running to incorporate. Season to taste with salt and pepper.

Charred Corn Relish

6 ears sweet corn, husked

Extra virgin olive oil

Kosher salt

Freshly ground black pepper

1 red bell pepper, roasted and diced

¼ cup red onion, diced

2 Tbsp cilantro, stems removed and chopped

1 lime, zested and juiced

Brush the ears of corn with extra virgin olive oil, season with salt and pepper, and place on the grill, turning every 2 minutes until all sides are nicely charred and kernels are just beginning to burst. Remove the corn from the grill with tongs and when the ears are cool enough to handle, cut the kernels off the cob with a sharp knife. Combine the corn with roasted pepper, diced onion, cilantro, and lime zest and juice in a mixing bowl. Mix well and season to taste with kosher salt and black pepper.

Red Pepper Aioli

1 red pepper

1 egg yolk

1 garlic clove

1 Tbsp red wine vinegar

3 dashes Tabasco

1 cup canola oil

Kosher salt

Freshly ground pepper

Roast red bell pepper according to the recipe (page 133). While the pepper is cooling, let egg come to room temperature. After pepper has cooled, remove the skin; remember not to wash

Roasted Game Hen with Honey Cumin Glaze and Warm Fingerling Potato Salad

Serves 4

2 Cornish game hens

2 Tbsp extra virgin olive oil

2 tsp Sundara Seasoning (recipe on page 136)

Honey Cumin Glaze (recipe below)

Warm Fingerling Potato Salad (recipe on page 62)

Preheat oven to 450° F. Place game hens breast side down on a cutting board. Using poultry shears or a sharp knife, cut from the neck to the tailbone to remove the backbone. Make a small slit in the cartilage at the base of the breastbone to reveal the keel bone. Grab the bird with both hands on the ribs and open up like a book, facing down toward the cutting board. Remove the keel bone. Cut each hen in half. Cut small slits in the skin of the bird behind the legs and tuck the drumsticks into them in order to hold them in place.

Heat a large cast iron pan on medium heat. Coat the bottom of the pan with olive oil. Generously season the hens with Sundara Seasoning and lay them skin-side down in the hot pan. Sear for 4 minutes on each side.

Pour ⅓ of the Honey Cumin Glaze on the bottom of a baking dish. Transfer the hens and their pan drippings to the baking dish. Pour the remaining glaze over the hens and place in the oven for 30 minutes or until a thermometer reaches an internal temperature of 165 degrees. Remove the dish from the oven and let them rest for about 5 minutes.

Honey Cumin Glaze

½ cup honey

2 Tbsp fresh orange juice

2 Tbsp fresh lemon juice

2 Tbsp balsamic vinegar

3 Tbsp cumin

3 Tbsp extra virgin olive oil

½ tsp kosher salt

½ tsp freshly ground black pepper

Place all ingredients into a mixing bowl and whisk until well incorporated. Can refrigerate for up to 7 days.

Roasted Game Hen with Honey Cumin Glaze.
This is one of the few dishes at Sundara that calls for heavy cream, but it is used in moderation. The glaze incorporates local honey and toasted cumin, a magical marriage that gives it a sweet and smoky Southwest flavor. Serve with warm fingerling potato salad.

Warm Fingerling Potato Salad

2 cups heavy cream

4 Tbsp unsalted butter

2 Tbsp whole grain mustard

1 cup organic chicken stock

1 tsp kosher salt

½ tsp fresh ground black pepper

10 fingerling potatoes, pre-boiled and cut into small rounds

1 red bell pepper, sliced thin

10 green beans, pre-blanched

2 cups, loosely filled, fresh arugula

In a medium sauté pan, add first 6 ingredients and bring to a boil. Cook at medium heat for 15 minutes or until slightly thickened. The mixture should coat the back of a spoon. Add potatoes, bell pepper, and green beans and cook for 5 minutes. Add fresh arugula and toss to combine.

To plate: Divide the warm potato salad between 4 plates and top with a roasted hen.

DESSERT

Strawberry Soup with Pound Cake Croutons

Serves 4–6

1½ lbs frozen strawberries

1 pint plain organic yogurt

½ cup fresh squeezed orange juice

½ cup organic cane sugar

Pinch of cardamom

½ cup water

Prepared pound cake

Fresh whipped cream

1 vanilla bean, scraped of seeds

Whipped cream, for garnish

Blend strawberries in a blender until smooth, slowly add yogurt and keep blending. Pour strawberry mixture into a large bowl and add orange juice, sugar, cardamom, and water. Stir until well blended. Chill for at least 1 hour before serving.

Cut prepared pound cake into ½-inch cubes. Pour 1¼ cup of soup into bowl, garnish with 10 croutons and top each bowl with whipped cream.

Banana Nut Spring Rolls

Serves 6

12 spring roll wrappers

4 bananas, peeled and cut into 4 inch pieces

2 Tbsp cinnamon sugar

½ cup Candied Walnuts, finely chopped (recipe on page 130)

Canola oil

Powdered sugar for garnish

1½ cups Caramel Sauce (recipe on page 131)

Cinnamon gelato or vanilla bean gelato, optional

Make these one at a time, keeping the remaining spring roll wrappers covered while working with them, as that will keep them moist and easier to roll out. Place a spring roll wrapper on a work surface. Place 1 banana piece diagonally across the center of each wrapper. Brush the opposite side with water, top each banana with a sprinkle of cinnamon sugar and 1 Tbsp of chopped walnuts. Roll the wrapper over the banana and fold each side in and roll like an egg roll. Press the ends together to form a seal. Repeat with remaining bananas and wrappers until finished. Place them on a sheet pan and cover with plastic wrap and refrigerate for at least 2 hours prior to frying.

Pour enough canola oil in a heavy-bottomed saucepan; you will need about 3 inches of oil. Heat the oil to 350° F. Prepare in small batches, turning frequently until the egg rolls are nicely browned, approximately 2–3 minutes. Remove with a pair of tongs and let dry on a paper towel–lined plate. When cool enough to handle, cut each spring roll in half, garnish with powdered sugar and Caramel Sauce, and serve with cinnamon or vanilla bean gelato.

Key Lime Pie with Brown Sugar Crust

Serves 10

For the Crust:

2½ cups graham cracker crumbs

½ cup brown sugar

²/₃ cup unsalted butter, melted

For the Filling and Meringue:

6 eggs, separated

2 (14-oz) cans sweetened condensed
    milk

¾ cup fresh key lime juice (at Sundara
    we use Nellie and Joe's brand)

½ tsp vanilla extract

½ tsp cream of tartar

1½ cups organic cane sugar

Preheat oven to 300° F. Lightly coat a
10-inch springform baking pan with
cooking spray.

To make the crust:

In a medium bowl, combine the graham
cracker crumbs and brown sugar. Pour
the melted butter over the crumb
mixture and stir with a spoon until evenly
combined. Pour about 2 cups of the
crumb mixture in the springform pan.
Tilt the pan and press the mixture along
the sides, turning the pan as you go,
until the crumbs are evenly packed up
the sides of the pan. Pour the remaining
crumb mixture into the pan and press

evenly in the bottom. The entire pan
should be coated with a ¼-inch crust.

To make the filling:

Place the egg whites in a large mixing bowl
and chill until needed. Meanwhile, in a
separate mixing bowl, beat the egg yolks
and sweetened condensed milk until well
combined. Slowly add the lime juice, then stir
in the vanilla extract while continuing to whisk
or beat the mixture until the ingredients are
well combined. Pour the filling into the crust
and set aside (the filling will begin to set).

To make the meringue:

Whip the egg whites with a kitchen mixer until
foamy. Add the cream of tartar and whip until
well combined. Add the sugar and beat on
high until the egg whites are very stiff,
3–5 minutes. Drop the meringue by large
spoonfuls over the filling. Working from the
outside in, smooth the top of the filling with a
spoon or offset spatula. Use a spoon to press
down lightly into the meringue and pull up,
forming peaks.

Bake for 25–30 minutes until meringue is
lightly browned. Remove from oven and cool
for 15 minutes; transfer to refrigerator and chill
for 3–4 hours before serving.

Fresh Mint Cheesecake with Watermelon Salsa

Serves 10

Filling:

2 envelopes unflavored gelatin

1 cup organic cane sugar

2 cups boiling water

1 lb cream cheese, room temperature

1 tsp vanilla extract

2 oz crème de menthe

½ cup fresh mint leaves, julienned

Mix gelatin and sugar in small bowl. Add boiling water and stir until gelatin is completely dissolved. Beat cream cheese and vanilla in a large bowl with electric mixer on medium speed until creamy. Gradually add gelatin mixture, crème de menthe, and mint leaves and beat until well blended. Pour into pie crust. Refrigerate 3 hours or until firm.

Pie Crust:

2 cups Oreo Cookie crumbs

½ cup unsalted butter, melted

Mix and press into 10-inch springform pan.

Watermelon Salsa

2 cups watermelon, ¼-inch diced

8 mint leaves, julienned

¼ cup Simple Syrup (recipe on page 135)

Pinch of kosher salt

Mix all ingredients in a small bowl and refrigerate until needed. Serve on the side.

Fall: Live In Harmony.

This is the culinary team's favorite time of the year. We love receiving the bushels of squash, potatoes, and beets from our farm partners. The smell of apples and apple cider sends us over the moon. It's duck season, and the salmon are running in the Midwest. If you're thinking comfort food, you'd be right on the mark. As fall concludes, the holidays commence, with our Thanksgiving menu a tribute to the vast emotions that go along with reconnecting over food.

Fall

Creamy Polenta with Mascarpone

Serves 4

6 cups cold water

2 cups polenta

¼ cup organic cane sugar

1 tsp kosher salt

8 Tbsp unsalted butter

2 cups mascarpone

In a large saucepan add cold water and polenta, stir well. Cook polenta on high heat until water is absorbed, approximately 20 minutes. Turn off heat and add sugar, salt, butter, and mascarpone. Serve immediately.

Sundara Signature Granola

Serves 10–12

Sundara Signature Granola. We make this fresh every day at Sundara. Be sure to use the old-fashioned oatmeal and real maple syrup. Serve over yogurt, munch as a snack, or add milk for a great breakfast cereal.

Dry Ingredients:

4 cups oatmeal

½ cup sunflower seeds

½ cup almonds, slivered

¼ tsp kosher salt

1 tsp nutmeg

1 tsp ground cinnamon

Wet Ingredients:

½ cup maple syrup

¼ cup honey

¼ cup brown sugar

⅛ cup vanilla extract

Preheat oven to 325–350° F. In a large bowl, mix all dry ingredients together. Set aside. In a large stock pot, add all the wet ingredients and bring to a boil, stirring often. Be careful not to over boil, the sugar will burn and can overflow. Let mixture cool until it is lukewarm or until you're able to handle it. Add wet ingredients into the bowl with the dry ingredients and thoroughly mix together.

Pour mixture onto a baking sheet and press granola so it is flat. It is a good idea to use a non-stick baking mat or wax paper on the bottom of the sheet pan as this makes removing it from the pan much easier. Bake for 30 minutes or until golden brown and firm. Depending on your oven, you may have to bake for additional time.

Once cool, crumble and store in an airtight container.

BEVERAGES

Beauty Smoothie

Serves 1

¼ cup grape juice
½ cup blackberries
¾ cup blueberries
½ cup pourable organic vanilla yogurt
½ cup cranberry juice

Place grape juice, blackberries, blueberries, yogurt, and cranberry juice in a blender and blend until smooth. For a better result, freeze the blueberries and blackberries overnight before adding to the recipe. If you choose not to freeze the fruit beforehand, you may add a ½ cup of ice.

Caramel Apple Martini

Serves 1

Caramel Sauce for rim of glass (recipe on page 131)
1 Tbsp cinnamon sugar
3 oz apple vodka
1 oz apple schnapps
2 oz apple juice
Ice

Rim glass and swirl the inside of the glass with caramel sauce. Sprinkle cinnamon sugar on the rim. Add all ingredients to shaker with ice; shake and strain into martini glass.

Autumn Smoothie

Serves 1

¼ cup granola
½ cup fresh squeezed orange juice
½ cup pourable organic vanilla yogurt
½ banana, peeled

Place granola, orange juice, yogurt, and banana in a blender and blend until smooth. For a better result, freeze the banana overnight before adding to the recipe. If you choose not to freeze the fruit beforehand, you may add a ½ cup of ice.

Autumn Smoothie. This could just as easily be called an autumn "soothie." Start your morning with this meal in a glass, it's loaded with B12.

Earth Smoothie

Serves 1

½ cup fresh blueberries

1 banana, peeled

½ cup almond milk

½ cup apple juice

Place blueberries, banana, almond milk, and apple juice in blender and blend until smooth. For a better result, freeze the blueberries and banana overnight before adding to the recipe. If you choose not to freeze the fruit beforehand, you may add a ½ cup of ice.

Rhythm Smoothie

Serves 1

¼ cup fresh cranberries

½ cup raspberries

3 large strawberries

½ cup pourable organic vanilla yogurt

½ cup cranberry juice

Place the cranberries, raspberries, strawberries, yogurt, and cranberry juice in a blender and blend until smooth. For a better result, freeze the cranberries, strawberries, and raspberries overnight before adding to the recipe. If you choose not to freeze the fruit beforehand, you may add a ½ cup of ice.

Pear of Roses Cocktail

Serves 1

Ice

2 oz Square One Botanical Spirits Vodka

3 tsp prickly pear purée

3 tsp Lavender Simple Syrup (recipe below)

2 Tbsp fresh squeezed orange juice

2 oz club soda

Long rosemary sprig, for garnish

Fill a tall hurricane glass with ice, then pour in vodka, pear purée, simple syrup, and orange juice. Stir with a long bar spoon. Top with club soda and garnish with rosemary sprig.

Lavender Simple Syrup

1 cup water

1 cup organic cane sugar

2 Tbsp fresh lavender flowers

In a medium saucepan, bring the water and sugar to a boil. Turn down the heat and add the lavender leaves. Simmer for 15 minutes, remove from stove and pour into a storage container. Leave the lavender in the syrup, the flavor will become stronger over time. Store for up to one month. Strain before using.

Spiced Apple Cider

Serves 8–12

- 2 quarts fresh apple cider
- 2 Tbsp brown sugar
- 4 whole cloves
- 2 cinnamon sticks
- 1 orange, sliced into rounds

In a large saucepan place all ingredients and cook on low heat to infuse the flavors. Strain and place in a coffee urn or punch bowl and serve warm.

Sundara Flirtini

Serves 1

- Ice
- 1½ oz Death's Door Vodka
- ¾ oz Cointreau
- 2 Tbsp cranberry juice
- 2 Tbsp pineapple juice
- 2 Tbsp dry champagne
- Orange twist, for garnish

Fill a bar shaker with ice and pour in vodka, Cointreau, juices, and champagne. Shake well and pour into a chilled martini glass. Garnish with an orange twist.

APPETIZERS

Goat Cheese Log

Serves 6–8

- 1 (11 oz) log goat cheese
- 2 oz cream cheese
- 4 tsp fresh chives, chopped
- 4 tsp fresh basil, chopped
- 4 tsp fresh parsley, chopped
- 1 tsp kosher salt
- ½ tsp freshly ground black pepper

Place goat cheese and cream cheese in a mixing bowl. Fold the cheeses together by hand. Add herbs, salt, and pepper and continue to fold together until well mixed. Roll the cheese between your palms to form a cylinder. Wrap tightly with clear plastic wrap and place in the refrigerator for at least 4 hours prior to serving. Serve with roasted beets and asparagus.

Mascarpone Stuffed Fresh Figs

Serves 8–9

- 1 pint fresh figs
- ½ cup mascarpone cheese
- 1 Tbsp heavy cream
- ¼ tsp vanilla extract
- 1 tsp powdered sugar
- Drizzle of Balsamic Vinegar Reduction (recipe on page 128)
- ¼ cup Candied Walnuts for garnish (recipe on page 130)

De-stem and wash figs, cut in half lengthwise and set aside. In a small mixing bowl, combine mascarpone cheese, heavy cream, vanilla extract, and powdered sugar and mix with rubber spatula until well blended. Place in a pastry bag and squeeze the mixture evenly over the figs. Drizzle with balsamic reduction and garnish with chopped Candied Walnuts.

Oven Baked Goat Cheese

Serves 2–4

1 Tbsp extra virgin olive oil

4 garlic cloves, minced

1 small white onion, diced

6 oz goat cheese

1 vine-ripened tomato, seeded and diced

1 Tbsp fresh cilantro, stems removed and chopped

1 Tbsp fresh parsley, chopped

¼ tsp Sriracha hot sauce

¼ tsp kosher salt

¼ tsp fresh ground black pepper

Preheat oven to 350° F. Heat olive oil in a sauté pan, then add garlic and onion and cook over medium heat until the onions have turned translucent, approximately 3–4 minutes. Transfer mixture to a mixing bowl to cool to room temperature. Add remaining ingredients to the bowl and mix with a rubber spatula. Pour mixture into an oven-safe bowl and bake for 15 minutes or until the mixture is hot and slightly browned on top. Serve with pita crisp or a warm baguette.

Roasted Beet Skewers with Balsamic Reduction

Serves 10–12

2 large roasted red beets (recipe on page 132)

8 spears blanched asparagus

1 herb goat cheese log (recipe on page 77)

24 skewers

Drizzle of Balsamic Vinegar Reduction (recipe on page 128)

Cut roasted beets into ½-inch cubes and set aside. Cut asparagus spears into 4 pieces. Divide goat cheese log into 24 (½ oz) pieces, and roll into balls. Place asparagus on the skewer first, then the goat cheese ball and finally the roasted beet on the bottom. Make sure you have a nice flat bottom of the skewer so it stands on end. Top skewer with rosemary stalk. Drizzle balsamic reduction on the bottom of the plate and then stand beet skewers on the plate.

Roasted Beet Skewers. The balsamic adds "yang" tang to the "yin" sweetness of the beets. Pair with crusty bread for scooping up the balsamic. Sip a pinot noir.

SOUPS AND SALADS

Acorn Squash Bisque

Serves 6

2 medium acorn squash

1 Tbsp canola oil

1 small white onion, chopped

2 cups organic vegetable stock

2 Tbsp brown sugar

½ tsp kosher salt

¼ tsp fresh ground black pepper

1 tsp cinnamon

1 (12 oz) can coconut milk

Pumpkin seeds and cinnamon, for garnish

Preheat oven to 350° F. Wash squash, cut in half and remove seeds. Place squash (cut side down) on baking sheet and bake for 50–60 minutes until squash is tender, let cool before next step. Use a slotted spoon to remove the pulp from the skin. In a large saucepan, heat oil over medium heat. Add onions and cook until translucent. Add squash pulp and vegetable stock. Cook over medium heat until mixture starts to boil, stir frequently. Stir in brown sugar, salt, pepper, and cinnamon. Remove from heat and let cool slightly. Using a hand blender, purée the soup. Return the pan to the stove and add the coconut milk and heat through. Garnish with pumpkin seeds or cinnamon.

Bacon Braised Brussels Sprouts

Serves 8

½ lb Nueske's smoked applewood bacon

1 small red onion, diced

2 lbs Brussels sprouts, cleaned and cut in half

2 cups organic chicken stock

2 Tbsp unsalted butter

Kosher salt

Freshly ground black pepper

Dice bacon into small pieces, about ¼ inch. Place bacon in a large sauté pan and cook over medium heat until crispy. Remove bacon from pan and place on paper towel–lined plate and set aside.

Return sauté pan to stove and add red onion and Brussels sprouts and cook until slightly browned. Add chicken stock and turn down to simmer, cover and cook for 10–12 minutes. Strain the Brussels sprouts and onions and return back to sauté pan. Add in the butter and bacon and toss until butter is melted. Season with salt and pepper to taste.

Butternut Squash Bisque

Serves 6–8

1 large butternut squash
1 Tbsp canola oil
1 Tbsp unsalted butter
½ cup onion, diced
¾ cup carrots, diced
3 cups organic vegetable stock
1 tsp kosher salt
½ tsp white pepper
½ tsp ground nutmeg
2 tsp ground cinnamon
¼ tsp fresh sage
¼ cup heavy cream, optional

Preheat oven to 350° F. Cut squash in half lengthwise and remove seeds. Place skin side up in a roasting pan and cook for 45 minutes until soft and caramelized. Allow to cool slightly.

Heat the oil and melt the butter in a large pot over medium heat. Cook the onion in the butter and oil until tender. Scoop out the cooked squash and add to pot along with the carrots. Pour in vegetable stock and season with salt, pepper, nutmeg, cinnamon, and sage. Bring to a boil, reduce heat, and simmer until vegetables are tender.

In a blender or food processor, purée the soup mixture until smooth. Return the purée to the pot and stir in the heavy cream. Heat through but do not boil. Serve warm.

Cabbage Slaw with Apples and Spiced Pecans. Go with Granny Smith apples to bring in the tart, with the Spiced Pecans bringing in the sweet.

Cabbage Slaw with Apples and Spiced Pecans

Serves 6

1 Tbsp apple cider vinegar
1 Tbsp organic cane sugar
¼ cup low-fat mayonnaise
2 cups cabbage, shredded
1 green apple, cored and sliced
2 Tbsp green onions, sliced
½ cup Spiced Pecans (recipe below)
Kosher salt
Freshly ground black pepper

Combine the vinegar, sugar, and mayonnaise until well mixed. Add the cabbage, sliced green apple, green onions, and Spiced Pecans. Salt and pepper to taste.

Spiced Pecans

1 cup organic cane sugar
1 tsp kosher salt
1 tsp ground cinnamon
1 pound whole pecan halves

Preheat oven to 300° F. In a bowl, mix together sugar, salt, and cinnamon. Add pecans to sugar mixture, mixing until well coated. Spread evenly onto a foil-lined cookie sheet. Bake for 15 minutes. Remove from oven and separate pecans as they cool.

Chicken and Red Grape Salad

Serves 4

- 2 cups chicken, cooked and cubed (poached in chicken stock)
- 1 cup seedless red grapes, halved
- 1 green apple, unpeeled and finely diced
- 4 Tbsp slivered almonds, toasted
- ½ cup celery, chopped

Dressing:
- ½ cup low-fat mayonnaise
- 1 Tbsp honey
- 1 Tbsp fresh lemon juice
- 2 Tbsp fresh basil, julienned
- ½ tsp celery salt

Combine chicken, grapes, apple, almonds, and celery in a medium bowl, set aside. Combine the mayonnaise, honey, lemon juice, basil, and celery salt in a small bowl and whisk thoroughly. Toss the dressing with the salad and serve.

Cranberry Chutney

Serves 6–8

- 1 pound fresh cranberries, rinsed
- 1 cup organic cane sugar
- ½ cup brown sugar
- ½ cup raisins
- 2 tsp ground cinnamon
- 1½ tsp ground ginger
- ¼ teaspoon ground allspice
- 1 cup water
- 1 cup sweet onion, chopped
- 1 cup Granny Smith apples, skin on, chopped
- ½ cup celery, chopped

Combine cranberries, sugars, raisins, spices, and water; cook over medium heat until juice is released from cranberries, about 15 minutes. Stir frequently. Add remaining ingredients and reduce heat to simmer. Cook for 20 minutes until thickened.

Mango Salmon Salad with Mango Vinaigrette

Serves 1

Mango Salmon Salad with Mango Vinaigrette. Salmon is the freshest in the fall and we source ours from the Midwest.

- 4 oz piece of fresh salmon, grilled
- Salt
- Pepper
- 4 cups fresh spinach, loosely filled
- 2 Tbsp red onion, julienned
- ¼ cup grape tomatoes
- ¼ cup cucumbers, diced
- ¼ cup mango, diced
- ¼ cup plus 2 Tbsp Mango Vinaigrette
- 2 Tbsp toasted almonds, for garnish

Season salmon with salt and pepper and spray with non-stick oil. Place on grill and cook to desired doneness, 3–5 minutes per side. Mix remaining ingredients in metal bowl with Mango Vinaigrette and place in the middle of a salad plate. Place cooked salmon on top of greens and garnish with toasted almonds.

Mango Vinaigrette

- 1 mango, peeled and cored
- 1 lime, zested and juiced
- 1 Tbsp fresh cilantro, stems removed and chopped
- 1 tsp organic cane sugar
- ⅓ cup rice wine vinegar
- 1 tsp honey
- 1 tsp Dijon mustard
- 1 cup blended oil (canola and olive oils)
- Kosher salt
- Freshly ground black pepper

Place all ingredients in blender except for the oil, pulse for 2 minutes and then slowly add the oil to create emulsion. Salt and pepper to taste. Refrigerate for up to 7 days.

Roasted Beet Salad

Serves 2

2 large roasted beets, peeled and
   sliced into ¼-inch thick slices
   (recipe on page 132)
1 herb goat cheese log, sliced into
   ¼-inch thick slices (recipe on
   page 77)
Drizzle of Balsamic Vinegar Reduction
   (recipe on page 128)
1 Tbsp toasted pine nuts, for garnish
Kosher salt
Freshly ground black pepper

Prepare the roasted beets, then
peel and slice the beets ¼-inch
in thickness. Shingle a beet slice
and alternate with a goat cheese
slice. When you are done shingling
the beets and goat cheese, drizzle
balsamic reduction over the salad
and garnish with toasted pine nuts
and salt and pepper.

Roasted Beet Salad.
Here's another idea—add
asparagus to the bottom of a
plate, drizzle with balsamic and
then layer the beets on top.

Wisconsin Beer Cheese Soup

Serves 8

4 Tbsp unsalted butter

1 cup carrots, small dice

1 cup celery, small dice

1 cup yellow onion, small dice

1 Tbsp garlic, minced

4 Tbsp white unbleached flour

1 tsp Tabasco sauce

1 Tbsp kosher salt

½ tsp freshly ground black pepper

2 cups organic chicken stock

1 bottle Miller Lite or other light beer

2 cups organic whole milk

1 tsp Dijon mustard

2 tsp dry mustard

2 tsp Worcestershire sauce

1 lb shredded Wisconsin sharp
   cheddar cheese

Cheddar popcorn, for garnish, optional

Wisconsin Beer Cheese Soup.
HINT: Light beer works best in this
soup. Try a Wisconsin microbrew to
keep it authentic.

In a large 6-quart pan, melt butter and add carrots, celery, onions, and
garlic. Cook until transparent, approximately 5 minutes. Add flour and
cook for 5 minutes. All flour should be absorbed by the vegetables. Add
Tabasco sauce, salt, pepper, chicken stock, and beer and cook for 15
minutes until slightly thickened. Add milk, Dijon mustard, dry mustard,
and Worcestershire sauce. Stir again. Add cheddar cheese and cook until
completely melted. Serve with cheddar popcorn as a garnish if you like.

ENTRÉES

Hanger Steak

Serves 4

1 cup soy sauce

6 Tbsp organic cane sugar

6 garlic cloves, minced

2 Tbsp sesame oil

2 tsp red pepper flakes

¼ cup organic ketchup

4 pieces hanger steak, about 4–6 oz each

Mix first 6 ingredients in a metal bowl until well blended. Pour over hanger steak, making certain all sides have been marinated. Cover and marinate for at least 12 hours.

Cook hanger steak on a char grill until desired temperature is reached. Slice on the bias and serve immediately.

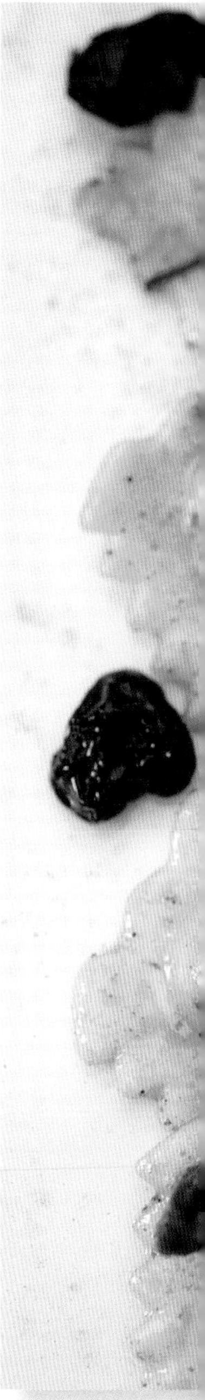

Butternut Squash Ravioli with Brown Butter and Sage

Serves 2

16 pieces butternut squash ravioli
8 Tbsp brown butter
½ cup Candied Walnuts (recipe on page 130)
½ cup Wisconsin dried cherries
4 fresh sage leaves, julienned
¼ tsp kosher salt
Freshly ground black pepper to taste
Sprinkle of fresh cinnamon

Bring a medium saucepan of water to boil. Add butternut squash ravioli and cook until its starts to float, about 5–7 minutes. While the pasta is heating, place the brown butter into a large sauté pan over medium heat. Once the butter is hot, strain the ravioli and add to the sauté pan, cook for 2 minutes. The ravioli will get a nice toasted texture on the outside. Add walnuts, dried cherries, and sage, toss again, and season with salt and pepper. Divide ravioli between two plates and sprinkle with cinnamon.

Butternut Squash Ravioli with Brown Butter.
This is such a favorite at Sundara. We use fresh sage from our gardens and dried cherries from Wisconsin's Door County peninsula.

Pan Seared Duck with Sun-Dried Cherry Risotto

Serves 4

4 duck breasts, 6–8 oz each
Kosher salt
Freshly ground black pepper
Sun-Dried Cherry Risotto
  (recipe opposite)
Port Wine Shallot Demi Glaze

Preheat oven to 325° F. Place duck breast fat-side up on cutting board. Score each side with a very sharp knife, cutting into the fat but not through the meat of the breast. Score in a criss-cross pattern on each breast. Use an oven-safe sauté pan or skillet, and heat skillet to medium-high heat. Season each breast on both sides with salt and pepper, add a little more salt to the fat side to help dry it out and achieve a crispier texture. Cook the duck skin-side down for about 4–5 minutes or until the skin is a nice golden brown. Remove some of the extra drippings in the bottom of the pan. Place pan in oven for 8–10 minutes until the duck is medium-rare or 130° internal temperature. Remove pan from oven and set the duck on a clean cutting board and allow to rest for 10 minutes. Slice each breast on the bias and serve with Risotto and Demi Glaze.

Port Wine Shallot Demi Glaze

2 Tbsp organic unsalted
  butter
2 large shallots, diced
2 Tbsp red wine vinegar
4 Tbsp honey
1 cup Wollersheim Port or
  your favorite port wine
1 tsp kosher salt
10 oz prepared demi glaze

Melt butter in a sauté pan on medium heat. Sauté shallots in butter until translucent, approximately 5 minutes. Add red wine vinegar and honey and allow to dissolve. Add wine and reduce by half. Add salt and demi glaze and cook for 15 minutes. Serve immediately.

Pan Seared Duck with Sun-Dried Cherry Risotto. The balance of sweet and sour in the sauce opens up the taste buds as you transition to the al dente risotto and succulent duck. Be sure not to overcook the duck.

Sun-Dried Cherry Risotto

Serves 6–8

  8 cups organic vegetable stock
  4 Tbsp extra virgin olive oil
  1 medium yellow onion, diced
  2 cloves garlic, minced
  2 cups Arborio rice
  1 cup Wollersheim Prairie Fumé or
      your favorite dry white wine
  1 tsp kosher salt
  ½ tsp white pepper
  1 cup Wisconsin dried cherries

Place vegetable stock in a large saucepan and heat to a simmer. Keep warm on the back of the stove. In a large heavy saucepan, pour olive oil and sauté onion and garlic until they turn translucent, approximately 2–4 minutes. Add Arborio rice to the pan and stir with wooden spoon and cook for another 3 minutes. Add the wine and allow the rice to absorb all the wine.

Start adding 1 cup of vegetable stock at a time, waiting for the rice to absorb the stock in between ladles. After you have added all of the stock, remove from heat and add salt, pepper, and cherries. Serve immediately.

DESSERT

Apple Cider Bread Pudding

Serves 12

8 large eggs

6 cups heavy cream

2 cups fresh apple cider

2 cups packed light brown sugar

4 Tbsp unsalted butter, melted

1 tsp kosher salt

1 tsp ground cinnamon

12 cups cubed stale bread (Texas Toast
    or leftover baguettes work well)

3 Granny Smith apples, peeled, cored,
    and cubed (about 3 cups)

Hard Cider Sauce

Preheat oven to 300° F. In a large bowl, beat the eggs. Add the cream, cider, brown sugar, butter, salt, and cinnamon and whisk to combine. Add the bread and apples, stir to combine. Pour into 9x13-inch pan, cover with plastic wrap and refrigerate until the bread is well saturated, up to 1 hour. Bake until the top is golden brown and the center is firm, about 1 hour. Remove from the oven and let sit on a wire rack for 15 minutes. Cut into pieces and drizzle with Hard Cider Sauce. Serve immediately.

Hard Cider Sauce

8 Tbsp unsalted butter

1 cup organic cane sugar

1 cup hard cider

8 large egg yolks

In the top of a double boiler, melt the butter over simmering water. Add the sugar and whisk to combine, whisking for 1 minute. Add the cider and whisk until the sugar is dissolved, about 2 minutes. Remove from heat and add the egg yolks, one at a time, whisking constantly. Return to the heat and continue whisking until the sauce is pale and slightly thickened, about 5 minutes.

Coconut Pudding

Serves 8

 1 cup organic whole milk
 1 cup coconut milk
 1 vanilla bean, sliced and seeded
 ¾ cup organic cane sugar
 10 Tbsp cornstarch
 Toasted coconut, for garnish, optional (recipe on page 134)

Pour milks into a saucepan and bring to a simmer, add vanilla bean with the seeds and allow to steep for 5 minutes. Turn heat to low and add sugar and cornstarch. Keep stirring until mixture starts to thicken. Remove vanilla bean pod and pour into 8 small serving bowls and chill for 2 hours before serving. Garnish with toasted coconut if you like.

Apple Walnut Date Tart

Serves 10

Date and Walnut Crust:

1½ cups dates, pitted

2½ cups walnuts

Filling:

1 lemon, juiced

2 cups water

3 Granny Smith apples, peeled and cored

½ cup apple juice

2 Tbsp honey

¼ cup dried Wisconsin cherries

¼ tsp ground cinnamon

⅓ tsp allspice

⅛ tsp ground cloves

Cinnamon Whipped Cream (recipe opposite), for garnish

To make the crust, place the pitted dates and walnuts into a food processor and pulse to a coarse texture. Remove the mixture from the processor and press into the bottom of a parchment-lined springform pan or tart pan. Refrigerate for 1 hour.

To make the filling, in a large bowl squeeze the lemon juice into the water and set aside. Slice apples into ¼-inch slices, and place in the water/juice mix. Drain apples and place in a large skillet. Add apple juice, honey, dried cherries, cinnamon, allspice, and cloves. Cook over medium heat for 10 minutes, stirring frequently.

Remove apples and cherries with a slotted spoon and allow to cool. Reduce remaining liquid in pan by half, remove from heat and allow to cool. Arrange apples decoratively on top of the walnut date crust and brush with the liquid. Allow to cool for 2 hours before serving.

Cinnamon Whipped Cream

1 cup heavy whipping cream
¼ cup organic cane sugar
½ tsp ground cinnamon
1 tsp vanilla extract

Pour whipping cream into a stand mixer or use a hand mixer
if you like. Whip the cream until it is almost stiff. Add sugar,
cinnamon, and vanilla and beat until the cream holds its peak.

Apple Walnut Date Tart. This no-bake tart gets its sweetness from
the natural sugars in the dates and apples, with just a touch of sugar
added to the apples to formulate a syrup. Serve with cinnamon
whipped cream.

Pumpkin Cheesecake

Serves 10

2 envelopes unflavored gelatin

½ cup organic cane sugar

½ cup brown sugar

2 cups boiling water

1 lb cream cheese, room temperature

1 tsp vanilla extract

½ tsp nutmeg

½ tsp allspice

1 tsp ground cinnamon

1 lb pumpkin purée

Mix gelatin and sugars in small bowl. Add boiling water; stir 5 minutes or until gelatin is completely dissolved. Beat cream cheese and vanilla in large bowl with electric mixer on medium speed until creamy. Gradually add gelatin mixture, spices, and pumpkin purée. Beat until well blended. Pour into pie crust (recipe opposite). Refrigerate 3 hours or until firm.

Pie Crust

8 Tbsp unsalted butter

2 cups gingersnap cookie crumbles

1 tsp organic cane sugar

½ tsp ground cinnamon

Preheat oven to 350° F. Place butter into a medium saucepan, cook over low heat to melt. In a separate bowl, place gingersnap cookie crumbs, sugar, and cinnamon and mix well. Slowly add melted butter to crumb mix and stir with a wooden spoon. Press mixture into the bottom of a 9-inch springform pan. Bake for 10–12 minutes until the crust is set. Allow to cool before adding pie filling.

Winter: Energize Your Soul.

If you're winter-averse, just think of this season as an extension of fall. All the root vegetables are being put to good use. Goat cheese seems to go really well with our winter menu. Our soups warm the soul, as do the pastas and meats. To say nothing of the three different kinds of hot chocolate we serve—spicy, sweet, and traditional— with guests especially enjoying a mug while cozying up to the fire pit adjacent to our heated outdoor infinity pool. In the spirit of full disclosure, we do import some fruit, but thoughtfully, as our thoughts turn to planning the perfect spring garden.

Winter

BREAKFAST

Almond Fruit Granola

Serves 10–12

- 1 cup brown sugar
- 1 cup unsalted butter
- ½ cup honey
- 2 Tbsp vanilla extract
- 2 Tbsp almond extract
- 4 cups raw oats
- 2 cups crispy rice cereal
- 1 Tbsp cinnamon
- 2 cups almonds, sliced
- 1 cup pecans
- 2 cups raisins
- 1 cup dried apples
- 1 cup dried Wisconsin cherries
- 1 cup dried apricots, diced
- 1 cup toasted coconut

Preheat oven to 350° F. Combine the sugar, butter, honey, and both extracts in a saucepan. Heat over medium heat until the butter is melted and the sugar has dissolved. In a separate bowl combine oats, rice cereal, cinnamon, almonds, and pecans; mix well. Fold the melted butter and sugar mixture into the oat mixture until well coated. Pour onto large cookie sheets and spread evenly, about ½-inch thickness. Bake for 20–25 minutes or until well toasted. Stir several times while cooking to ensure even browning. Remove from oven and allow to cool on the cookie sheets for 30 minutes. After granola has cooled, place in a large mixing bowl and stir in the dried fruits and coconut. Store in a tightly covered container for up to 4 days.

Blue Cornmeal Pancakes with Pine Nuts and Lingonberries

Serves 4–6

1½ cups blue cornmeal, medium grind

2 tsp kosher salt

2 Tbsp organic cane sugar

2 cup boiling water

1 cup organic whole milk

2 eggs, beaten

4 Tbsp unsalted butter, melted

1½ cups unbleached white flour

4 tsp baking powder

½ cup pine nuts

Wisconsin maple syrup

Lingonberry preserves

In a medium bowl, mix together the blue cornmeal, salt, and sugar. Stir in the boiling water until all of the ingredients are wet. Cover and let stand for a few minutes. Combine the milk, eggs, and melted butter. Stir the milk mixture into the cornmeal mixture. Combine the flour and baking powder. Stir into the cornmeal mixture until just mixed. If the batter is stiff, add a little more milk until the batter flows off of the spoon thickly but smoothly. Stir in the pine nuts.

Heat a large cast iron skillet over medium heat, and grease it with a dab of oil or butter. Use about 2 Tbsp of batter for each pancake. When the entire surface of the pancake is covered with bubbles, flip over and cook until golden.

Serve with Wisconsin maple syrup and lingonberry preserves.

Blue Cornmeal Pancakes. The blue cornmeal adds a nice texture to these pancakes. Serve with a side of bacon for a smoky complement to the sweetness of the pancakes and the slightly sourness of the Swedish lingonberries.

Irish Steel Cut Oatmeal with Peaches

Serves 4

8 cups water

2 cups steel cut oats

4 Tbsp brown sugar

2 cups chopped frozen peaches

Bring water to a boil and add oats. Leave the burner on high and boil the oats until they just begin to thicken. This will take about 5–8 minutes. Stir the oats every few minutes and scrape the bottom of the pot if they begin to stick. You will be able to hear the oats popping as they boil.

Reduce the heat to a low simmer. Allow the oats to cook for about 30 minutes, stirring every few minutes. Do not worry if the oats begin to stick to the bottom of the pot. Continue to stir and at some point near the 30-minute mark, they usually stop sticking.

After the oats have cooked for 30–35 minutes, remove from heat. An ideal consistency is thick and creamy, but not dry. Stir in brown sugar. Add the peaches and stir until completely mixed.

B12 Magic Coffee

Serves 1

1 Tbsp organic cocoa powder
2 Tbsp Grade B maple syrup
Freshly brewed coffee of your
choice

Grab your favorite coffee mug and place the cocoa powder and maple syrup in the bottom of the cup. Stir the two ingredients together to form a paste to ensure proper mixing in the coffee. Fill the mug with hot coffee and enjoy.

B12 Magic Coffee.
We call this the "morning magic ritual." By adding Grade B maple syrup and organic cocoa powder to your morning coffee, you are actually giving yourself a shot of B12 to start the day, which helps regulate hormone levels and keeps you feeling less stressed from morning to night.

Coconut Tres Leches Hot Chocolate

Serves 8

>6 cups organic skim milk
>2 (14 oz) cans unsweetened coconut milk
>1 (14 oz) can sweetened condensed milk
>4 Tbsp good quality unsweetened cocoa powder
>2 vanilla beans, cut in half lengthwise
>Whipped cream, for garnish
>Chocolate shavings, for garnish

In a medium saucepan, combine all three milks and simmer over medium heat. Stir occasionally to keep from burning. Whisk in cocoa powder until well incorporated. Add vanilla beans (make sure to cut beans in half and add seeds to the milk). Let simmer for 5 more minutes, remove vanilla beans and pour in mugs. Top with whipped cream and chocolate shavings if desired.

Hot Buttered Rum

Serves 1 (Rum batter made in bulk)

Rum Batter:

2 tsp ground cinnamon
1 lb unsalted butter
2 tsp vanilla extract
2 lbs brown sugar
2 tsp cardamom

Add all the ingredients to a food processor and blend until smooth. Place mixture in a freezer-proof container until needed.

Making the drink:

Grab your favorite coffee mug and add a shot of your favorite rum, add 2 Tbsp of frozen rum batter and top with hot water.

Passion Smoothie

Serves 1

½ banana, peeled
½ cup prickly pear purée
½ cup pourable organic vanilla yogurt
½ cup fresh squeezed orange juice

Place all ingredients in a blender and blend until smooth. For a better result, freeze the prickly pear purée and banana overnight before adding to the recipe. If you choose not to freeze the fruit beforehand, you may add a ½ cup of ice.

Savory Smoothie

Serves 1

¼ cup pumpkin purée
¼ cup Sundara Signature Granola (recipe on page 71)
½ banana, peeled
½ cup pourable organic vanilla yogurt
½ cup whole organic milk
Ground cinnamon, for garnish

Place pumpkin, granola, banana, yogurt, and milk in a blender and blend until smooth. For a better result, freeze the bananas and pumpkin purée overnight before adding to the recipe. If you choose not to freeze the fruit beforehand, you may add a ½ cup of ice. Garnish with cinnamon, if desired.

Spicy Hot Chocolate

Serves 4

4 cups organic skim milk

2 cups heavy whipping cream

2 cinnamon sticks

2 star anise

1 cup organic cane sugar

1 vanilla bean, cut and scraped
of seeds

½ lb organic dark chocolate,
cut into chunks

1 tsp dry chili flakes

Marshmallows, for garnish

Combine the milk and cream, add the cinnamon and star anise. Refrigerate the mixture overnight. The next day pour mixture into a large saucepan and bring to a simmer over medium heat. Add the sugar and vanilla bean and cook for 5 minutes or until the sugar is dissolved. Remove the star anise, vanilla bean pod, and the cinnamon sticks with a slotted spoon. Whisk in the chocolate and chili flakes and cook until chocolate has fully melted into the milk mixture. Pour into mugs, top with marshmallows and enjoy.

Spicy Hot Cocoa. Soak the spices in the milk overnight to help infuse the flavors into the milk. You can use pre-made marshmallows but we thought it would be fun to make our own. We cut a large three-inch round marshmallow to cover the entire surface of the drink—it melts evenly and gives you some marshmallow goodness in every sip.

Sundara Organic Hot Cocoa

Serves 14

> 2 cups organic cane sugar
> 1 cup dry milk powder
> 1/3 cup organic cocoa powder
> ½ tsp kosher salt
> ½ tsp cardamom
> ½ tsp cinnamon
> ½ tsp nutmeg
> 1 vanilla bean, scraped of seeds

In a mixing bowl add all ingredients and mix well. Keep covered in cool dry place. Add 4 Tbsp dry mixture to 1½ cups hot water.

Note: When working with vanilla bean, split the bean in half lengthwise. With a spoon or knife, scrape out the seeds and add the seeds to the dry mixture; discard the vanilla pod.

The Cure All

Serves 1

> Ice
> 1.5 oz organic vodka
> Dash of bitters
> ½ lime, juiced
> ¼ cup peach purée
> ½ cup grapefruit soda
> Lime wedge, for garnish

Fill a pint glass with ice and add vodka, bitters, lime juice, and peach purée. Stir with a bar spoon and top with grapefruit soda. Garnish with a lime wedge.

APPETIZERS

Bacon Wrapped Bleu Cheese-Stuffed Dates

Serves 4–6

12 large Medjool dates, pitted

6 oz Carr Valley Ba Ba Bleu cheese

6 slices Nueske's applewood smoked bacon

Preheat oven to 350° F. Slice each date in half, being careful not to slice all the way through the date. You want to form a pocket into which you'll stuff the cheese. Place ½ oz of bleu cheese inside each date and pinch date back together. Cut each piece of bacon in half and wrap one piece around each date, securing the bacon with a toothpick. Sear each side of the stuffed date in a hot sauté pan until bacon is golden brown. Cook the dates on a cookie sheet until the dates have browned nicely, 10–15 minutes. Turn the dates halfway through the cooking process to ensure even browning.

Black Bean Purée

Serves 2–4

1 cup dry black beans

5 cups water, divided

1 Tbsp red wine vinegar

2 tsp canola oil

1 large garlic clove

2 Tbsp fresh cilantro, stems removed

6 grape tomatoes

½ tsp cumin

¼ tsp kosher salt

¼ tsp freshly ground black pepper

Place black beans in 2 cups of water and let sit overnight. The next day, rinse beans to remove any dirt and unwanted beans. Cook beans in 3 cups of water for 90 minutes or until softened. Strain beans and place in a food processor. Add remaining ingredients to the food processor and pulse until well puréed. Serve immediately with crusty bread or as a dip with fresh vegetables.

Chicken Lettuce Wraps with Ponzu Dipping Sauce

Serves 8–10

4 boneless skinless chicken breasts

Chicken stock

2 Tbsp blended oil (canola and olive oils)

1½ cups trumpet mushrooms

3 Tbsp green onions, chopped

2 tsp garlic, minced

1 tsp ginger, minced

2 cups water chestnuts, diced ¼ inch

1 cup Ponzu Dipping Sauce (recipe below)

1 head iceberg lettuce

Poach chicken breasts in chicken stock until fully cooked. Remove from stock and chill chicken for 30 minutes before dicing. Dice chicken into ¼-inch pieces and set aside. Add blended oil to sauté pan and sauté mushrooms, green onions, garlic, ginger, and water chestnuts for 5 minutes. After sautéing, pour ingredients over chicken and toss with Ponzu Dipping Sauce.

To assemble:

Take 1 head of iceberg lettuce and remove core by placing it core side down and firmly smashing it on the cutting board. Turn the lettuce head over and the core should pull out easily. Cut the head of lettuce in half and gently pull back each layer separately. These will be the leaves used as the wraps. Spoon chicken mixture into each lettuce cup and fold over like a burrito. You may use remaining Ponzu sauce for dipping.

Ponzu Dipping Sauce

¼ cup organic cane sugar

½ cup water

2 Tbsp soy sauce

2 Tbsp rice wine vinegar

2 Tbsp organic ketchup

1 Tbsp fresh lemon juice

$\frac{1}{8}$ tsp sesame oil

1 Tbsp hot mustard

2 tsp water

1-2 tsp garlic and red chili paste

Place all ingredients in medium bowl and mix, cover, and chill.

Black Bean Soup

Serves 8

1 Tbsp extra virgin olive oil

3 slices Nueske's bacon, rough chopped

½ cup green peppers, seeded and diced

¾ cup onions, diced

2 Tbsp garlic

1 (12 oz) bottle light beer like Miller Lite

2 tsp Tabasco sauce

4 (15 oz) cans black beans

½ cup water

1 Tbsp dry sherry

¼ tsp ground cumin

Kosher salt

Freshly ground black pepper

Heat oil in a pot over medium heat. Add the chopped bacon and sauté for 1 minute. Add the peppers, onions, and garlic, and sauté for 2 minutes. Add the beer and Tabasco sauce, bring to a boil. Add 3 cans of beans with their juice and bring back to a boil. Pour in blender or food processor and purée the soup until smooth. Return mixture to pot, add the water and remaining 1 can of beans and bring back to a boil. Add the sherry, cumin, and season to taste with salt and pepper.

Cinnamon Yam Mash

Serves 8

> 5 lbs yams, peeled, diced into 2-inch pieces
> 2 quarts water, hot
> 1 Tbsp kosher salt
> 16 Tbsp unsalted butter, cold, ½-inch dice
> 1½ tsp ground cinnamon
> ¼ tsp white pepper
> ½ cup brown sugar

Place the peeled and diced yams in a large stockpot. Add hot water and salt, and place the stockpot on the stove over medium heat. Bring to a boil and cook for 35 minutes or until a fork inserted into the yams pierces easily.

Drain the water and transfer yams to a mixing bowl. Using a potato masher, mash until yams are broken up. Add diced cold butter, ground cinnamon, white pepper, and brown sugar, then mix again until the yams are smooth and all the ingredients are mixed evenly. If needed, season with additional salt to taste.

Sweet Potato Salad

Serves 12

Dressing:

¼ cup extra virgin olive oil

2 Tbsp pure maple syrup

2 Tbsp fresh orange juice

2 Tbsp balsamic vinegar

1 Tbsp fresh lemon juice

2 tsp fresh ginger, peeled and minced

½ tsp ground cinnamon

¼ tsp ground nutmeg

Combine all ingredients and chill.

Salad:

6 pounds sweet potatoes, peeled, cut into ¾-inch cubes

1 cup green onions, chopped

1 cup fresh parsley, chopped

1 cup pecans, toasted, coarsely chopped

¾ cup dried Wisconsin cherries

Steam sweet potatoes in batches until potatoes are just tender, about 10 minutes per batch. Transfer sweet potatoes to a large bowl; cool to room temperature. Add green onions, parsley, pecans, and cherries. Pour dressing over; toss gently to blend.

Sweet Potato Salad. This tasty salad is a true celebration of fall in Wisconsin. We add cherries, maple syrup, and fall spices to bring out the sweetness in the sweet potatoes. Try it for breakfast!

Wisconsin Stravecchio Garlic Mashed Potatoes

Serves 8–10

- 4 lbs Wisconsin russet potatoes (do not peel)
- 1 cup organic skim milk
- 1 cup organic unsalted butter
- 2 cloves garlic, minced
- 1 Tbsp kosher salt
- ½ Tbsp freshly ground black pepper
- 4 oz shredded Wisconsin Stravecchio cheese

Wash and quarter potatoes. Add to a large pot of boiling water and cook for approximately 15–20 minutes. While potatoes are cooking, place milk, butter, and garlic in a small pot and cook over medium heat until butter is melted and milk is hot. Drain potatoes. Using a hand mixer, a standing mixer, or a good ol' fashioned potato masher, mash potatoes into desired consistency, add hot milk mixture and continue to mash. Then add salt, pepper, and shredded cheese. Serve immediately.

ENTRÉES

Grilled Salmon with Chai Tea Risotto

Serves 4

> 1 lb Irish organic salmon filets, 4 oz each
> ½ tsp Sundara Seasoning (recipe on page 136)
> 8 oz shiitake mushrooms, sliced
> 1 cup Mirin Broth (recipe below)
> 4 portions Chai Tea Risotto (recipe opposite)

Irish organic salmon thrives off the pristine waters along Ireland's western coastline. You can special order this from your local fishmonger. Sprinkle each piece of salmon with Sundara Seasoning and grill on each side for 4–5 minutes. This salmon is best served medium-rare.

Place shiitakes in a medium saucepan along with the Mirin Broth and cook until mushrooms are soft and have been well marinated, approximately 8–10 minutes.

Cook Chai Tea Risotto according to the recipe and place grilled salmon over the top of the risotto. Divide the poached mushrooms among the four plates and drizzle a little of the poaching liquid onto the salmon.

Mirin Broth

> ¾ cup soy sauce
> ½ cup mirin rice wine
> 7 Tbsp organic cane sugar
> 1 tsp grated fresh ginger
> 1 tsp minced garlic
> 2 cups organic chicken stock
> 2 Tbsp rice wine vinegar or white wine vinegar
> 1½ tsp Asian sesame oil
> 1 sheet of nori, cut into matchsticks

Combine all ingredients in a mixing bowl and refrigerate.

Chai Tea Risotto

Serves 8

6 cups organic vegetable stock

1 cup chai tea concentrate

4 Tbsp extra virgin olive oil

1 medium yellow onion, diced

2 cloves garlic, minced

2 cups Arborio rice

1 cup Wollersheim Prairie Fumé wine or
    your favorite seyval blanc wine

1 tsp kosher salt

½ tsp white pepper

Place vegetable stock and chai tea concentrate in a large saucepan and heat to a simmer. Keep warm on the back of the stove. In a large heavy saucepan, pour olive oil and sauté onion and garlic until translucent, approximately 2–4 minutes. Add Arborio rice to the pan and stir with wooden spoon and cook for another 3 minutes. Add the wine and allow the rice to absorb all the wine. Start adding 1 cup of vegetable stock at a time, waiting for the rice to absorb the stock in between ladles. After you have added all of the stock, remove from heat and add salt and pepper. Serve immediately.

Grilled Salmon with Chai Tea Risotto. A NOTE FROM CHEF JOHN: This recipe is a lesson in serendipity. I was at home making risotto and discovered my wife had used the last of the chicken stock. I found chai tea concentrate and figured, why not, and it became one of those happy mistakes in my culinary journey. The risotto takes on a Christmas flavor— think soothing and warm—plus it's fairly sweet without any added sugar. I like to get out the grill in the winter and grill the salmon.

Oven Roasted Pork Loin with Polenta and Pickled Apples

Serves 4

2 lbs pork tenderloin, cleaned and silver skin removed
1 Tbsp extra virgin olive oil
1 Tbsp Sundara Seasoning (recipe on page 136)
Mascarpone Polenta (recipe below)
Pickled Granny Smith Apples (recipe opposite)

Preheat oven to 500° F. Rub tenderloin with olive oil. Sprinkle Sundara Seasoning over pork. Place pork in a 9x13-inch dish. Bake pork for 15 minutes. Turn oven off, but do not open the oven door. Let pork sit in oven for 45–60 minutes longer, until meat thermometer reads 145 degrees. Move to cutting board and allow to sit for 5 minutes before slicing into 16 pieces.

Mascarpone Polenta

6 cups water
2 cups polenta
¼ cup organic cane sugar
1 tsp kosher salt
8 Tbsp unsalted butter
2 cups mascarpone

In a large saucepan, add cold water and polenta, stir well. Cook polenta on high heat until water is absorbed, approximately 20 minutes. Turn off heat and add sugar, salt, butter and mascarpone. Serve immediately.

Pickled Granny Smith Apples

4 Granny Smith apples
1 lemon, juiced
1 red onion, thinly sliced
2 Tbsp fresh dill, chopped
2 cups apple cider vinegar
4 bay leaves
1 tsp whole black peppercorns
1 tsp kosher salt
⅔ cup organic cane sugar

Quarter the apples, then cut away core and thinly slice. In a medium bowl, squeeze lemon over the top of the apple slices, then add the onions and dill. In a small pot over medium heat, add the vinegar, bay leaves, peppercorns, salt, and sugar. Stir and heat until the sugar has completely dissolved. Pour evenly over the apples and let stand 20 minutes, turning occasionally. Serve or cover and refrigerate until ready to use.

To plate:
Divide polenta between 4 plates, shingle 4 pieces of roasted pork loin on polenta. Use a slotted spoon to place the pickled apples on top of the pork loin.

Marechal Foch Braised Short Ribs. We use a wine from nearby Wollersheim Winery called Domain Du Sac, made from an on-premise-grown grape called Marechal Foch. This ruby red wine with deep flavors of raspberry, cherry, and oak is a perfect match for the short ribs.

Marechal Foch Braised Short Ribs

Serves 4

2 Tbsp vegetable oil

8 short ribs, trimmed of extra fat

Kosher salt

Freshly ground black pepper

White unbleached flour, for dredging

2 onions, ¼-inch dice

2 carrots, peeled, ¼-inch dice

2 ribs of celery, ¼-inch dice

8 cloves garlic, minced

2 Tbsp tomato paste

1 bottle Marechal Foch wine

2 quarts beef broth

4 sprigs parsley

4 sprigs thyme

1 sprig rosemary

2 bay leaves

Preheat the oven to 350° F. In a large Dutch oven, heat the oil over medium heat. Season the ribs with salt and pepper and dust lightly with the flour. Sear the ribs in the oil, in batches if necessary, until well-browned on all sides, 4–5 minutes per side. Remove from pan and set aside. Lower the heat to medium and add the onions, carrots, celery, and garlic. Sauté the vegetables for 5–7 minutes, or until lightly browned. Add the tomato paste and cook for 2 minutes.

Add the wine, ribs, beef broth, and herbs to the pot. Bring to a boil, cover tightly, and place in the oven (or leave on the stove on simmer) to braise for 3½–4 hours or until the ribs are very tender. Skim and discard the fat that rises to the surface.

Transfer the ribs to a platter; keep warm. Boil the liquid left in the pot until it has reduced to 1 quart. Season with salt and pepper and pour through a fine mesh sieve; discard the solids.

At this point, the ribs and the sauce can be kept covered in the refrigerator for 2–3 days. Reheat gently, basting frequently. Serve ribs over creamy polenta or buttered pasta.

DESSERT

Bleu Cheese Cheesecake with Poached Pears

Serves 12

For Poached Pears:

1 bottle Port wine (at Sundara, we use Wollersheim)

1 cup organic cane sugar

1 sprig fresh rosemary

1 orange rind

1 vanilla bean, split and scraped

6 medium pears

For the Cheesecake:

16 oz cream cheese, room temperature

10 oz Wisconsin Hook's Bleu Cheese, room temperature, finely crumbled

3 eggs, room temperature

¼ cup sour cream

2 Tbsp honey, clover or orange variety

Pinch of kosher salt

Pinch of freshly ground black pepper

Candied Walnuts (recipe on page 130), for garnish

Honey, for garnish

To make the poached pears:

In heavy sauce pot, combine all ingredients except pears; bring to a boil. Cook until reduced by one-fourth. Meanwhile, peel pears and add peels to poaching liquid. Cut pears in half and core. Once reduced, strain poaching liquid and add pears. Bring to a simmer and poach pears until tender. Place pears and liquid in opaque container. Cover with plastic and let stand at room temperature overnight.

To make the cheesecake:

Preheat oven to 250° F. Spray an 8-inch springform pan with cooking spray. Line bottom with parchment paper; spray again. In a large bowl, beat cream cheese until smooth. Add bleu cheese, beat until creamy. Add eggs one at a time, beating well after each addition.

Scrape bowl. Add sour cream, honey, salt, and pepper. Beat until combined. Pour into pan. Bake 40–45 minutes or until set and knife inserted near center comes out clean. Cool at room temperature overnight in pan.

To assemble:

Remove cheesecake from pan. Cut into 12 pieces. Place one piece of cheesecake on a plate and add 1 piece (half) of the poached pear. Garnish with Candied Walnuts and a drizzle of honey if desired. Refrigerate leftovers.

Bleu Cheese Cheesecake with Poached Pears. Living in Wisconsin brings you a variety of culinary treats, with some of the best known delicacies being our artisan cheeses. We use a bleu cheese that is produced less than 30 miles away and pairs extremely well with our Wollersheim Winery port-poached Wisconsin pears.

Flourless Chocolate Torte with Vanilla Bean Crème

Serves 10

Cocoa powder for dusting pan

½ cup water

1 tsp kosher salt

¾ cup organic cane sugar

18 oz bittersweet chocolate, finely chopped

1 cup unsalted butter, cut into small pieces

6 large eggs

1 tsp vanilla extract

Crème Anglaise (recipe opposite), for garnish

Powdered sugar, for garnish

Fresh raspberries for garnish

Preheat oven to 300° F. Grease a 10-inch round pan and dust with cocoa powder; set aside. In a small saucepan combine water, salt, and sugar and cook over medium heat until dissolved, set aside.

In a double boiler melt the bittersweet chocolate. After the chocolate is melted, pour into the bowl of an electric stand mixer and add the butter one piece at a time. Beat in the hot sugar and water mixture. Now add one egg at a time and continue to mix until all the eggs are added.

Pour the batter into the prepared pan and spread it out evenly. Place pan in a larger pan to create a water bath. Fill the outside pan with enough water to come halfway up the pan. Bake until the torte puffs slightly and a toothpick inserted into the center comes out very moist but not liquid, about 40 minutes. Do not overcook. Transfer the pan to a wire rack and let cool for 30 minutes. After torte has cooled completely, cover and refrigerate until very cold, at least 4 hours or overnight. To remove the torte from the pan, dip the bottom of the cake pan in hot water for 15 seconds. Invert onto a serving platter. Garnish with Crème Anglaise, powdered sugar, and fresh raspberries.

Crème Anglaise

1 quart heavy whipping
  cream
½ cup white sugar
1 vanilla bean, split and
  scraped of seeds
6 egg yolks

In a saucepan combine
heavy cream, sugar, and
vanilla bean and seeds.
Bring to a simmer but be
careful not to let it boil;
turn off heat. Place 6 egg
yolks in a bowl and whip
until pale in color. Using a
2-oz ladle, carefully temper
the eggs by ladling 2 oz of
cream mixture at a time
into the bowl. Once eggs
are tempered, pour back
into saucepan and cook
over medium heat stirring
constantly until slightly
thickened. Strain liquid into
a quart container and allow
to cool before placing in
the refrigerator.

Winter Lemon Pudding Cake

Serves 8

¼ cup unsalted butter

1¼ cups sugar

Pinch of kosher salt

3 tablespoons Meyer lemon zest

6 egg yolks

6 Tbsp white unbleached flour

¼ cup freshly squeezed Meyer lemon juice

2 cups organic whole milk

8 egg whites

Preheat oven to 325° F. Cream the butter, sugar, salt, and lemon zest together in a mixing bowl. Add the egg yolks one at a time, mixing well after each addition. Add the flour and mix well. Add lemon juice and the milk and mix until combined. In a separate bowl, beat the egg whites to stiff peaks, then fold into the batter.

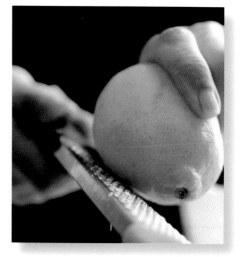

Immediately pour the batter into a plastic wrap–lined 9x13-inch pan and bake in water bath for 35–45 minutes or until golden brown and firm. Let cool and then invert onto a sheet pan and refrigerate to chill. Use a ring cutter to cut out eight 3-inch circles just prior to serving.

Juices

Juicing gives your digestive system a rest so your body can put its energy into cleansing, recovery, and healing. Some say they experience new energy, clearer complexion, and clarity of mind and body. Here is a sampling of the many types of juices we offer at Sundara for you to try at home.

JUICING TIPS FROM CHEF JOHN

- Make sure all vegetables and fruits are washed before using.

- Use a good quality juicer.

- Remove the peels from oranges, grapefruits, and lemons before juicing. All other fruits and vegetables do not have to be peeled before using.

- Always use organic produce when making juices. Drink immediately, as the nutrients will start to break down right away.

Apple-Lemon-Ginger

This juice is a great aid for digestion. It also helps cleanse the system of toxins.

2 Granny Smith apples, cored
1 lemon, peeled
1 oz ginger root, peeled

Apple-Mint-Coconut

The mint is the magic in this juice, as it calms the stomach, reduces headaches, and improves blood circulation.

1 Granny Smith apple, cored
6 mint leaves
¾ cup coconut water

Beet-Apple-Celery

Along with being a general tonic and cleanser, this juice helps ease stiff joints. It's high in iron, antioxidants, and Vitamin C.

1 celery stalk
1 Granny Smith apple, cored
1 red beet

Carrot-Beet-Celery

The combination of celery and carrots works like a shot of Vitamin K for bone health. It's also good for the overall health of your eyes and skin thanks to an abundance of Vitamin A.

1 celery stalk
2 carrots
1 red beet

Orange-Strawberry-Coconut

What's not to love about strawberries—they're delicious and a good source of Vitamin C, a nutrient that supports a healthy immune system and produces collagen for healthy skin. This is a refreshing, feel-good juice.

2 large strawberries, stems removed
2 oranges, peeled
¾ cup coconut water

Spinach-Lemon-Apple-Cucumber

Talk about a powerful anti-aging antioxidant-rich juice. It boosts your body's defenses against inflammation and damage to cells, two main causes of aging.

½ cup spinach
1 Granny Smith apple, cored
½ lemon, peeled
1 stalk celery
½ cucumber, skin on

Watermelon-Carrot-Apple-Celery

High in Vitamins A and C and full of antioxidants, watermelon is also very cleansing, hydrating, and refreshing.

1 celery stalk
1 Granny Smith apple, cored
1 carrot
8 pieces watermelon cut in 1-inch cubes

The Basics

Balsamic Vinaigrette

1½ cups canola oil

¼ cup balsamic vinegar

¼ cup whole grain mustard

1 tsp kosher salt

1 tsp freshly ground black pepper

2 Tbsp fresh basil

1 Tbsp fresh chopped parsley

2 cloves fresh garlic

¼ cup firmly packed brown sugar

Place all ingredients in a blender and purée until smooth. Refrigerate for up to 7 days.

Balsamic Vinegar Reduction

1½ cups balsamic vinegar

2 Tbsp brown sugar

2 Tbsp honey

1 orange, juiced

Place all ingredients into a heavy-bottomed saucepan. Bring mixture to a boil and then turn down to simmer for approximately 20 minutes. The vinegar will reduce by half. Remove from stove and allow to cool. Mixture will have a nice syrup-like consistency. This will keep for a month in a covered container. You do not need to refrigerate.

Blanched Asparagus

Before you blanch asparagus, make sure you have cleaned it by snipping off the bottom end of the asparagus where it is still white.

Bring a large pot of water to boil on the stove. While waiting for the water to boil, make the water bath: In a separate bowl place a tray of ice cubes and fill it with enough water to cover the ice. This will be used to bring down the temperature of the asparagus rapidly so it does not overcook.

When the water starts to boil, place the asparagus in the water and cook for approximately 3–5 minutes. This will depend on the thickness of the asparagus (our rule of thumb at Sundara is pencil size). After the asparagus has been blanched in the boiling water, remove it with tongs and place in the cold water bath for 5 minutes.

You can serve these immediately if you want them hot, or keep them in the refrigerator until needed.

Blanched Asparagus. Delicious as a side, we also include blanched asparagus in our roasted beet salad.

Bloody Mary Mix

1 quart organic tomato juice

1 lime, juiced

2 Tbsp horseradish

½ tsp kosher salt

½ tsp freshly ground black pepper

½ tsp celery salt

1 Tbsp Worcestershire sauce

¼ tsp Tabasco Sauce

Place all ingredients in a large bowl and whisk until well mixed. Refrigerate for at least 4 hours prior to use. Keeps for up to 7 days in the refrigerator.

Bloody Mary Mix. Admitting our bias, we do believe this makes the best Bloody Mary you'll ever taste.

Candied Walnuts

2 quarts water

3 cups organic cane sugar, divided

2 lbs walnuts

Preheat oven to 350° F. Combine 2 quarts water and 2 cups sugar and bring to a boil. Add walnuts and poach for 2 minutes in the water. Strain walnuts and shake to remove excess water. Place walnuts in a gallon plastic bag with remaining 1 cup of sugar and shake to coat. Spray sheet pan with nonstick spray. Bake walnuts until golden brown, approximately 15 minutes.

Candied Walnuts. These add a touch of sweetness to salads and they top our Butternut Squash Ravioli.

Caramel Sauce

2/3 cup brown sugar

2/3 cup organic cane sugar

2/3 cup light corn syrup

4 Tbsp unsalted butter

1 cup heavy cream

In a saucepan combine sugars, corn syrup, and butter. Cook, stirring constantly, over medium-high heat until mixture reaches a boil. Remove from heat and stir in cream.

Caramel Sauce. While you could go for store-bought, nothing beats homemade, especially with sweets.

HOW TO Brown Butter

1 lb unsalted butter

Place butter into a heavy-bottomed saucepan. Cook on medium heat until the butter starts to melt. Once it starts to bubble, start whisking. The butter will start to foam, keep whisking until you start to see little brown specs on the bottom of the saucepan. The butter should turn a nice caramel color and have the smell of toasted nuts. Turn off the heat and move the pan to a cool surface. Skim off any butterfat that has risen to the top. Use immediately or place in a covered container in the refrigerator.

Brown Butter. This adds a deep, nutty flavor to your food.

HOW TO Roast Beets

Roasting beets brings out the natural sugar and flavor in the beet.

Preheat oven to 400° F. To prep the beets, snip off the greens at the top of the beet. Rinse beets in cold water. Wrap each beet in tin foil and place on a cookie sheet. Roast in oven for 60–75 minutes. You should be able to stick a knife through them after they have been roasted.

Remove beets from oven and allow them to cool enough to handle. Peel each beet by pulling away the skin, similar to peeling the layers back from an onion. Beets can be kept in the refrigerator for up to one week.

Roasted Beets. Even for those of you who think you don't like beets, one taste of a roasted beet is a sure bet to change your mind.

HOW TO Roast a Red Bell Pepper

Wash the bell pepper and dry the skin. Turn gas burner on high heat and lay the pepper directly on the flame. That's right, directly on the grate, just where you'd put a frying pan.

The skin will start to burn in about 30 seconds. As the skin blackens, rotate the pepper so all sides are blackened. All the skin should be black, and the pepper will start to soften up. This process will take between 5–10 minutes.

Once completely black, remove the pepper from the stove and place in a paper bag. Fold the top of the bag over to seal it as tightly as you can (you can use plastic, but

let the pepper cool for a minute so you don't melt the plastic). The heat from the pepper will create steam. That steam causes the burnt skin to loosen up from the flesh of the pepper. Once cooled (about 10 minutes) remove the pepper, and with your hands (and maybe a paper towel) rub the skin off the pepper. It should come off quite easily, and you're left with the soft red flesh. A few bits of black here and there are fine, but you want most of it gone. Don't wash the pepper under water, as that will wash away a lot of the flavor.

Roasted Red Bell Peppers. Our Red Pepper Aoili depends on roasted peppers for its smoky flavor. Roasted peppers are also great in pasta dishes.

HOW TO Toast Coconut

You can toast coconut in the oven or on the stovetop.

To toast coconut in the oven, preheat oven to 300° F. Spread shredded coconut in a thin layer on a baking sheet. Bake for about 20 minutes, stirring every 5 minutes to make sure the coconut is browning evenly.

To toast coconut on the stovetop, spread shredded coconut in a large skillet and cook over medium heat, stirring frequently until coconut is mostly brown. Cool completely. Store in an airtight container until ready to use.

Toasted Coconut. Coconut is already delicious, we'll give you that, but toasting brings out the natural sweetness.

Oven Roasted Tomatoes

5 Roma tomatoes, cut in half and seeds removed

1 tsp minced garlic

4 sprigs fresh thyme, stem removed, or 1 Tbsp dried thyme

2 Tbsp balsamic vinegar

¼ cup olive oil

1 tsp organic cane sugar

1 tsp kosher salt

1 tsp freshly ground black pepper

Preheat oven to 275° F. Place tomatoes in a large bowl and add remaining ingredients. Toss well to cover the tomatoes with all the herbs and spices. Line a cookie sheet with parchment paper and place tomatoes cut-side up on the paper. Drizzle the remaining liquid from the bowl over the tomatoes. Roast for 45 minutes, remove from oven and let cool. Store in refrigerator in a covered container.

Oven Roasted Tomatoes. You'll never look back once you use roasted tomatoes in a Caprese Salad.

Sesame Lime Dressing

½ cup white vinegar

½ cup sesame oil

¼ cup soy sauce

1 lime, freshly squeezed

1 cup organic cane sugar

1 tsp dry mustard

1 tsp kosher salt

½ tsp white pepper

2 Tbsp sesame seeds

2 cups low-fat mayonnaise

The easiest way to prepare this recipe is in a stand mixer using a wire whip attachment. Place white vinegar, sesame oil, soy sauce, and lime juice in mixer and turn on low until well mixed. Add remaining ingredients and turn mixer on medium speed and mix until well blended and there are no lumps from the mayonnaise. Refrigerate for up to 7 days.

Sesame Lime Dressing. Great on all types of lettuce, from arugula to romaine, and it never wilts the lettuce.

Simple Syrup

1 cup water

1 cup organic cane sugar

Place water and sugar in a saucepan and cook over medium heat until the sugar has dissolved. Let cool and keep refrigerated in a covered container.

Simple Syrup. This is the base for all our signature mojitos.

Sundara Seasoning

1 cup kosher salt

¼ cup onion powder

¼ cup garlic powder

¼ cup paprika

¼ cup freshly ground black pepper

1 Tbsp cayenne pepper

Mix all ingredients together in a mixing bowl and store covered in a cool dry place. Use this seasoning for chicken, steaks, and any desired proteins.

Sundara Seasoning. Six ingredients—so simple, so versatile, so Sundara—to season the protein of your choice.

Tips, Trade Secrets, and Tidbits from Chef John

Always Use Kosher Salt. Kosher salt has a uniform texture, which makes it easy to season dishes. Kosher salt also has a less intense flavor than iodized salt.

Always Use Unsalted Butter. We always use unsalted butter in our recipes, as it's much easier to control your salt level with unsalted butter. Plus, it lasts longer than salted butter.

Fresh vs. Dried Herbs. We have been growing our own herbs at Sundara for years now. Use fresh, but don't add them until you're ready to serve the dish. The oils that carry most of the flavor will dissipate with more than 15 minutes of cooking, so add them last.

The Squeeze. One of the most oft-used items in our kitchen is the hand-held citrus juicer. We juice everything. We make our lemonade to order. Grapefruit, oranges, and limes are all juiced to order for our cocktails.

Organic Cane Sugar. Natural, organic cane sugars are less refined than commercial white sugars, often retaining a light tan color and counting about 10 percent cooked cane juice in a rich array of trace minerals. This also gives organic sugar a richer, multi-dimensional taste that enriches the flavor of any dish prepared with it.

Freshly Ground Black Pepper. Anything that has been cut, ground, or processed before you get it is not going to be as fresh. Do yourself a favor and buy a pepper mill—you will taste the difference.

Margarine. Don't use it, period. It literally is one molecule away from being plastic. It's extremely high in trans fat and increases cholesterol.

Grow Your Own. You will get such satisfaction from growing your own produce. Even if you're living in an apartment, put a little pot of herbs on the windowsill and cut them when you need them. Place a bigger pot on your balcony. It's good for you and the environment.

The War on Soda. I used to be a six-pack-a-day soda-holic until I put down the can and started reaching for the refillable bottled water. You will feel so much better when you are giving your body what it needs. Plus, it's a natural weight loss tool.

Support Your Local Farmer. Take advantage of a CSA (Community Supported Agriculture) by purchasing a share in the crop of a local farm. If a full share is too much, ask about a half share, or split it with your neighbors. You can even work at the farm to help pay for the share. So get acquainted with the soil and eat some great organic produce.

Smoothie Freeze. When making smoothies, always freeze the fruit you are going to use in the drink. This will eliminate having to add ice, which only waters down the smoothie, taking away some of the natural flavors with it.

Naked Food. Eliminate excess calories by using stocks or yogurt instead of cream. Use organic produce without all the pesticides. Your body will love it.

The Riches of Wisconsin

We take great joy in partnering with Wisconsin farms, wineries, breweries, artisan cheese makers, and more in developing our seasonal menus. Our guests appreciate it, too.

Orange Cat Community Farm. One of our CSA (Community Supported Agriculture) farm partners is Orange Cat Community Farm, located just a short drive from Sundara, where all the produce is grown without the use of synthetic pesticides and fertilizers.

"I was raised in the area and am excited to settle down on the land I know. Growing plants and cultivating a deep relationship with nature has always brought me immense joy. I want to share that joy with others. My goal is to create a place where others can develop a similar relationship with the land. What better way than through the food you eat!" —Owner Laura Mortimore

What is Community Supported Agriculture?
Community Supported Agriculture is a way to connect the consumer directly to the farmer who grows the food. Members purchase a share in the farm in exchange for weekly or bi-weekly boxes of produce. But it's much more than just that. It is an opportunity to support a local farmer, be introduced to new foods, get in touch with your environment by eating with the seasons, and create community with others who are sharing the same experience. By joining a CSA, you get something that many others don't—you know where your food comes from and how it was produced. It just tastes better that way.

Wisconsin Fruits. Our apples come from Lapacek Orchard in Poynette, our cherries from the Door County peninsula, and our cranberries from Warrens.

Gentle Breeze Honey, Mt. Horeb. Here's a family business that started out as a hobby and is now a full-time endeavor with 600 hives. Eugene and Donna Woller enlist the help of their children, too.

Dairy. Here in the Dairy State we turn to Sassy Cow Creamery in Columbus and the farms of Organic Valley for all our dairy products.

Carr Valley Cheese, La Valle. Another family-run business, Carr Valley Cheese is over one hundred years old, with master cheese maker Sid Cook at the helm. Sid has won more top national and international awards than any other cheese maker on the continent. You must try their Cocoa Cardona and Aged Cheddar.

"Carr Valley is very proud to have its artisan cheeses featured in this collection of healthful regional recipes, which balance seasonality, creativity, and passion into delicious flavor." —Master Cheese Maker Sid Cook

Hook's Cheese, Mineral Point. Begun in 1976 by college sweethearts Tony and Julie Hook, Hook's Cheese is located in a building built into the hills of Mineral Point some 150 years ago during the area's mining era. We fancy their Four-Year Cheddar Cheese.

BelGioioso Cheese, Green Bay. These are classic Italian cheeses made in Green Bay by Errico Auricchio. Errico's great-grandfather started a cheese company in Italy more than a century ago, and Errico started BelGioioso when he moved his family from Italy to America in 1979.

Nueske's Bacon, Wittenberg. The Nueske family ancestors came to Wisconsin in 1882, bringing with them their European skills in smoking, spicing, and curing meat. Their applewood-smoking recipes remain unchanged all these years later and they blend their spices by hand.

Wisconsin Microbreweries. We made a commitment to feature only Wisconsin brews on our beverage menu and that was a very good decision. Guests enjoy craft beers from New Glarus, Tyranena, Port Huron, Ale Asylum, Milwaukee Brewing, Steven's Point Brewing, Leinenkugel's, and Central Waters. We also feature Wisconsin distilleries like Death's Door, Old Sugar Distillery, and Yahara Bay.

Yahara Bay Distillers, Madison. Family owned and operated, Yahara Bay searches the state to find the best grains, fruits, and herbs cultivated by local growers to make their premium spirits. All of their products are handcrafted in small batches to ensure quality.

Wollersheim Winery, Prairie du Sac. This winery overlooking the Wisconsin River Valley beat out Napa Valley wineries for the 2012 Winery of the Year honors at the prestigious San Diego International Wine Competition. We love the tenacity of this family-run winery in producing fine wines from winter hardy hybrid varietals. The winery dates back to the 1840s when Hungarian Count Agoston Haraszthy, considered the "father of the American wine industry," first grew grapes here.

> *"Wollersheim Winery is thrilled to be associated with Sundara Spa. What a wonderful way to blend and marry locally grown food with locally made wines. It is part of the total experience of Wisconsin flavors."*
>
> —Winemaker Philippe Coquard

Index

Green Practices

Green Spa Network

Sundara is a seed member of the Green Spa Network, a non-profit organization that promotes the natural connection between personal well-being, economic sustainability, and the health of our planet.

Sundara is certified by Travel Green Wisconsin, a voluntary program designed to protect the beauty and vitality of the state's landscape and natural resources by certifying tourism businesses that have made a commitment to reducing their environmental impact.

Sundara participates in the Global Soap Project, gathering up discarded soap bars from our suites and providing them to the Global Soap Project to process into new soap bars that are then distributed to vulnerable populations throughout the world. It literally can mean the difference between life and death.

Supporting Breast Cancer Recovery

Sundara is committed to and supports Breast Cancer Recovery, a grassroots organization based in nearby Madison, Wisconsin, whose mission is to provide environments for women breast cancer survivors to heal emotionally. All programs are designed and conducted by survivors for survivors. Sundara is pleased to be a host of their Infinite Boundaries wellness retreats, where women learn and practice healing strategies to live life more fully. Sundara's spa therapists lovingly donate their time and talents during these retreats. Sundara also hosts an annual Golf & Spa Classic to benefit the organization. A portion of the proceeds of this book go to Breast Cancer Recovery. To learn more, visit bcrecovery.org.

Sundara Inn & Spa®

Accolades & Awards

#5 Destination Spa in the World
—Readers' Poll, *Travel + Leisure Magazine,* World's Best Spas for 2012

10 Best Boutique Hotel Spas in the World
—Readers' Choice, SpaFinder.com, 2011

Top 10 Spas in the Midwest
—*Spa Magazine,* 2010

#3 Favorite Spa Escape in America
—ABC's *"Good Morning America,"* 2006

Most Eco-Conscious Resort in America
—1st Annual Healthy Travel Awards, *SHAPE Magazine,* 2006

10 Great Eco-friendly Spas in the World
—*USA Today,* 2005

4 Groundbreaking Spas
—*CNN Headline News,* 2004